ELECTRONIC MAIL (E-MAIL)

1. MODULE CONTENTS:

1.1. MODULE OBJECTIVES

The teachers and teacher educators will be able to;

- Conceptualize the idea of electronic mails.
- Create an e-mail ID.
- Compose and draft the e-mails along with the attachment and links/ hyperlinks.
- Use advanced features of formatting e-mails and send them in different approaches.

1.2. INTRODUCTION

In this technological world, we are continuously changing our technical adaptation patterns in the race of becoming **tech-savvy**. Being a teacher, a constant pressure is always put on us to go online and use the available technological tools to make the teaching learning process more fruitful. So, in this module we will be discussing the use of an essential online facility which has significance in almost every part of our personal or professional life.

In your day-to-day life, you must have seen a postman carrying mails and letters and delivering them door to door. These mails include essential information required for you. But these days, mails can also be sent to people using your digital gadgets like smartphones, tablets, computers, or laptops. These mails are called as **electronic mails** abbreviated to **e-mail.** These are used to send important information to your desired person within a fraction of millisecond or second wherever in the world along with the files or documents.

E-mail according to its use is of two major types, namely personal e-mail, and professional e-mail.

Personal e-mail: These e-mails are free to create and can be used by anyone in and around the globe for their personal uses. The example of personal e-mail is Gmail, Yahoo, Rediff mail, Hotmail etc. with domain names like @gmail.com, @yahoo.com, @rediffmail.com, @hotmail.com etc.

Professional e-mail: These e-mails are generally purchased e-mails and is provided to the employees of a specific organization/ company/ universities/ institutions. Its domain example can be @microsoft.com, @bhu.ac.in, @flipkart.com etc.

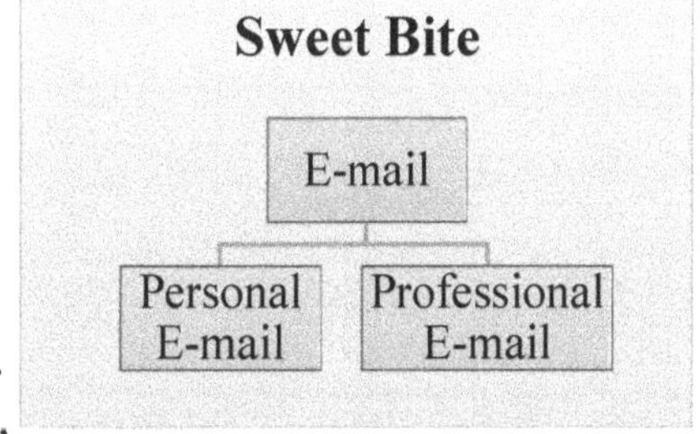

As we do not have much concern in the professional e-mail, we should now focus on the personal e-mails, their usability and applicability.

Need of e-mails for us as a teacher/ teacher educator:

After the COVID-19 pandemic, our classroom witnessed a drastic shift from rhetoric face-to-face teaching style to online learning style and different teaching learning approaches. In order to use different learning platforms, a valid e-mail ID is the first step towards it. A valid e-mail ID provides access to diverse resources online with a stable internet connectivity.

We can send information to our students & colleagues regarding the upcoming events, notify on upcoming classes, send important documents and files to all the students at once.

E-mail provides access to almost all mobile applications and websites. A few include,

These are only a few examples of what we can access, there is a lot more of things which can be accessed by us if we know how to use e-mails effectively to enhance our professional competencies.

So, let's see how we can use an e-mail to enhance our professional skills. But before we proceed to using e-mail and its features, let's first create an e-mail ID.

GMAIL:

There are a plenty of e-mail addresses' domains which can be used to create an e-mail address. A few have already been discussed above. Gmail is an official email service provided by the Company Google. Here, we will create an email ID using the Gmail facility with an extension of gmail.com.

WHY ARE WE USING IT?

Gmail is easily accessible and is available at free of cost. Gmail also provides access to various applications of Google like Google Drive, Google Photos, Google Meet and many more which we will be discussing in the upcoming module.

Salty Bite

We can't create an e-mail ID in which of the following extension/ domain?
(a) @gmail.com
(b) @yahoo.com
(c) @up.gov.in
(d) @rediffmail.com

You can click on this video if you want to know more about e-mail.

How to Create an E-mail ID?

Open Gmail application on your smartphone/ open a browser on your computer/ laptop (for example, Google Chrome, Microsoft Edge, Firefox, Opera Mini etc.) and search for Gmail on the search option.

For computers/ laptops, you can use this link: https://mail.google.com/mail/u/1/

Sweet Bite

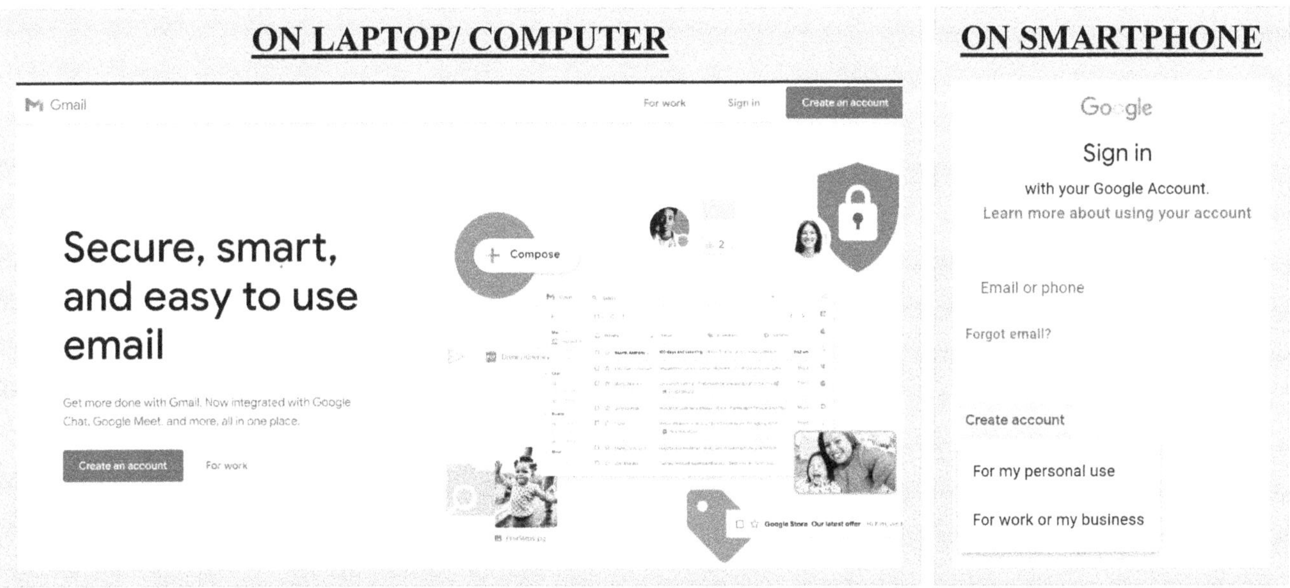

How Gmail looks like?

An interface like this will appear on your interface.

(In case of smartphone follow the step as:

Go to Gmail application → Click on Add Google account → Click on Add Google account → Click on Create account.)

Click on the sign "Create an account/ " and follow the steps accordingly.

ON LAPTOP/ COMPUTER

ON SMARTPHONE

If you face any difficulty in creating a Gmail account, here is our step-by-step companion to assist you create it.

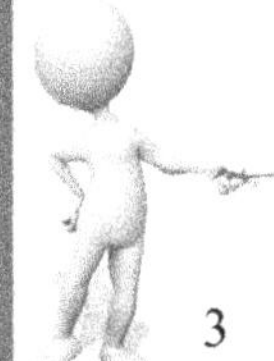

Step-by-step Guide to Create Gmail Account

Furthermore, you can also watch an interactive video by a Google product expert.

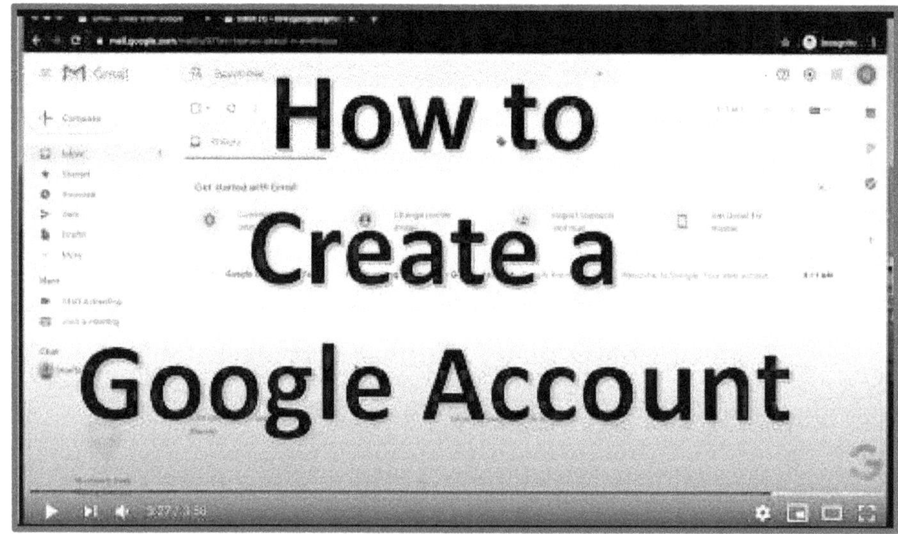

<u>What did we learn?</u>

1) Which of the following is a free domain extension?
   a) @gov.in
   b) @up.nic.in
   c) @outlook.com
   d) @microsoft.com
2) The OTP received on your phone number starts with which alphabet?
   a) G b) M c) E d) X
3) After all this account creation process, your username will be associated with which of the following?
   a) @hotmail.com
   b) @yahoo.com
   c) @gmail.com
   d) @rediffmail.com
4) If I don't want to give my mobile number for the creation of e-mail ID, I can skip it. (T/ F)
5) Why do we use e-mail these days?
   ....
   ....
   ....

As we have already created a valid e-mail address. Let's now see, what are the different functions of buttons provided to you on e-mail interface (main page of e-mail).

We will not look into all aspects of Gmail but only the parts necessary for us in teaching learning process. Let's first discuss all the important points of Gmail interface, then we will look into the images to get a better understanding of the functions.

⊢ **Compose-** In the composition option, we can type our e-mails, select the participants, write the subject of the e-mail, add files, attachments, links, and also edit the required fields and also send the formatted e-mail to the selected participants.

▣ **Inbox-** The inbox section of the Gmail stores the e-mails received from different sources. It primarily has three major labels under which the e-mails are stored. The primary section deals with all the necessary e-mails that needs our attention. It can be from the students, teachers, administrators, or colleagues. In the promotion label, the promotional advertisements are available. If a company, for example, Flipkart sends you an e-mail to purchase from their app, it is stored in the promotion label. In the Social label, all the communications from different social media platforms.

☆ **Starred-** The starred section generally accounts for the storage of e-mails which were star marked by us for some reason. In case, I don't need to search a specific e-mail in such a crowd of mails, instead I can easily switch to "starred" section and read the same.

◔ **Snoozed-** If we consider the same example given above, what if I forget to read that e-mail in such workload. To prevent it, I can simply put that e-mail on snooze mode. By this, that specific e-mail will automatically pop-up in my inbox interface at the time I mentioned during snoozing the e-mail.

➤ **Sent-** In this section, all the e-mails that we sent to others for different works are stored. This helps us in navigating through what was sent by us to whom and when was it sent.

◻ **Drafts-** Sometimes, while typing an e-mail, we often leave it mid-way due to some other work with higher priority. In such cases, all the incomplete mails are stored in the draft section. When we decide to resume our work on that e-mail, we can directly go to the draft section and continue from the section where I left off.

▷ **Important-** The e-mails which are important for us in the upcoming time, we can just mark them important.

▣ **Chats-** The chat option generally is for organizing a meeting with the colleagues or friends or students. Once we go to the chats tab, we can organize a meeting or interact.

➣ **Scheduled-** When we plan to send an e-mail at a specific time, say for example, it is 9 o'clock now and we want to send an e-mail of learning materials to our students at 11:00AM, we can still send the e-mail at 09:00AM but with scheduled mode. Here, we can select the date and time to send the e-mail, so that even if we forget to send the e-mail at a specific time, it can be sent without any hassle.

✉ **All Mails-** In this section, all types of received e-mails, including inbox and spam are displayed. The deleted e-mails won't be visible. If your Gmail account has more than one account signed in, we can see all the e-mails on a single interface.

⊘ **Spam-** Spam means an e-mail from an unknown source (which is not recognised by Gmail)

🗑 **Bin-** All the deleted e-mails are stored here. We can restore the deleted e-mails from the bin folder within 30 days, if it is deleted by mistake or is important.

▷ **Categories-** In the categories tab, the different categories of e-mails are stored. We can show or hide the categories in the Gmail, but categories can neither be created nor deleted. Different categories of Gmail include, Social, Updates, Forums and Promotions.

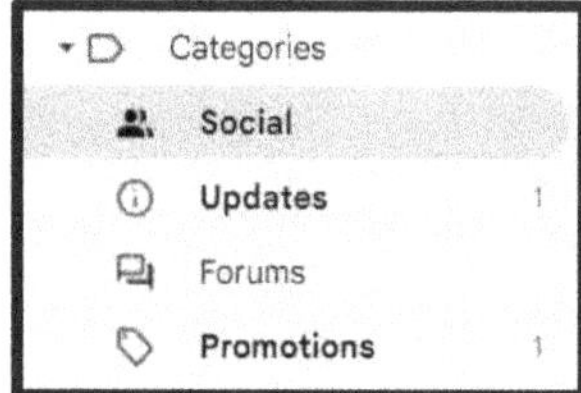

⚙ **Manage Labels-** In this section, labels like Inbox, Starred, Snoozed, Important, Chats, Sent, Scheduled, Drafts, All Mail, Spam, Bin, Categories, Social, Updates, Forums, and Promotions can be selected on whether to hide them or show them.

＋ **Create New Label-** If we want to create a new label in Gmail, for example, a label of Class X students to store all details of class X, we can create the same here.

🔍 **Search Mail-** The search mail option appears on top of the Gmail interface. Here we can search any e-mail using the e-mail subject/ sender's name/ sender's ID, or file name. Further, we can apply additional filters to find search results faster.

● **Profile icon-** You will find the option of signing out in the bottom of the interface after clicking on the profile icon. You will also have an option of **Manage your Google Account.** You can change the profile icon of your Google account by choosing **Personal Info** option. **Data and privacy** help you handle your data that are being shared in other platforms. The **Security** option manages Google account activity. **People and sharing** stores all your files and other details shared by you to others through e-mail. **Payments and subscriptions** manage all your purchases.

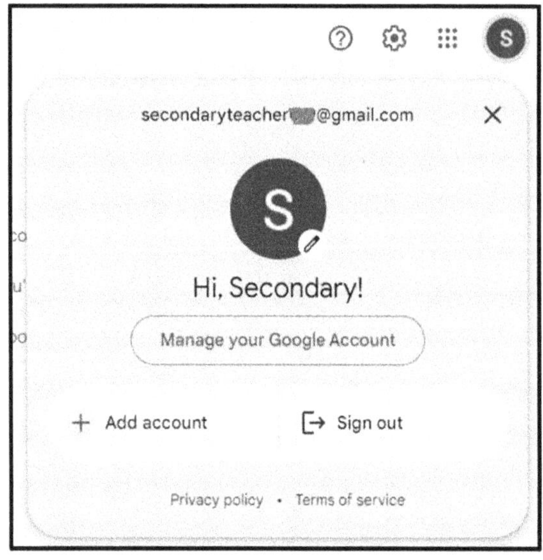

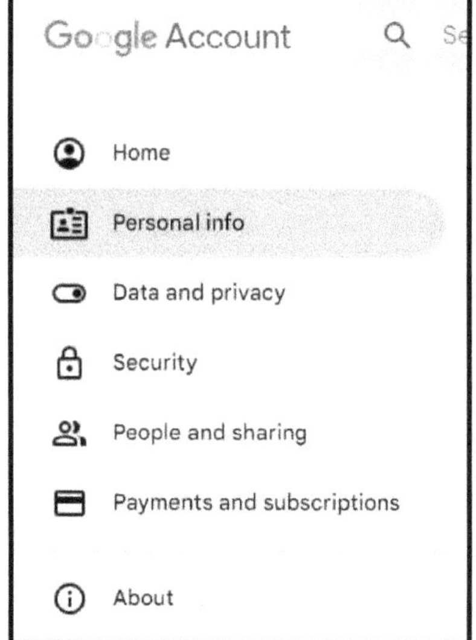

Pictorial Interpretation of Gmail Interface are as follows:

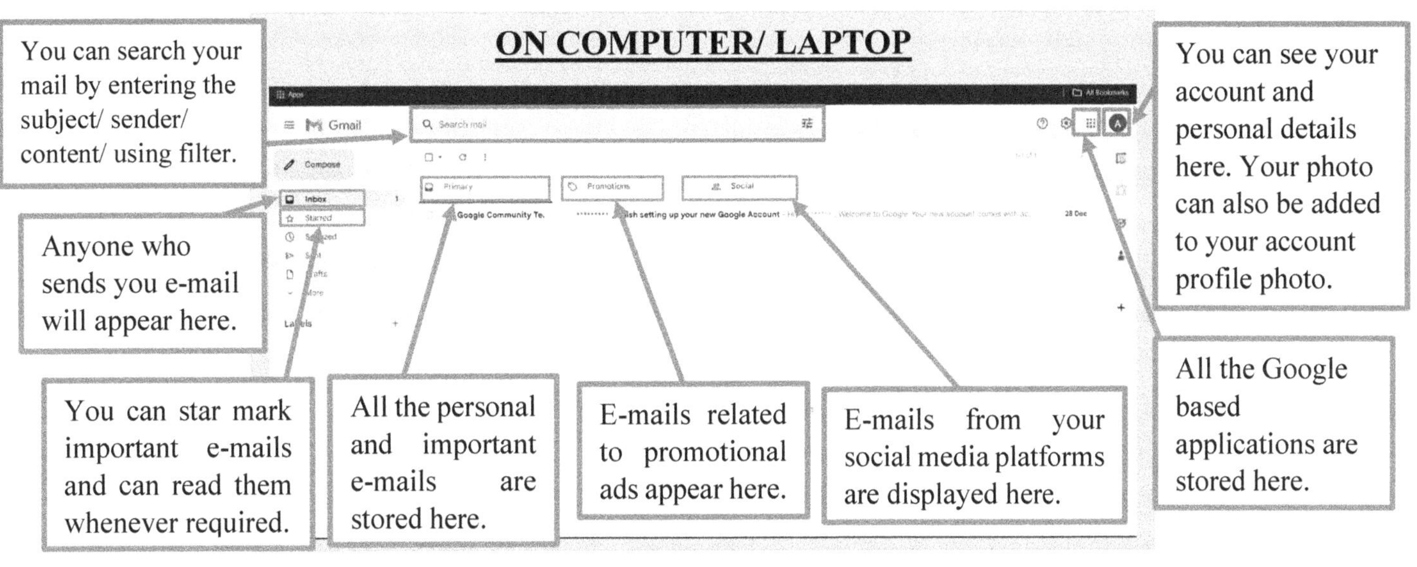

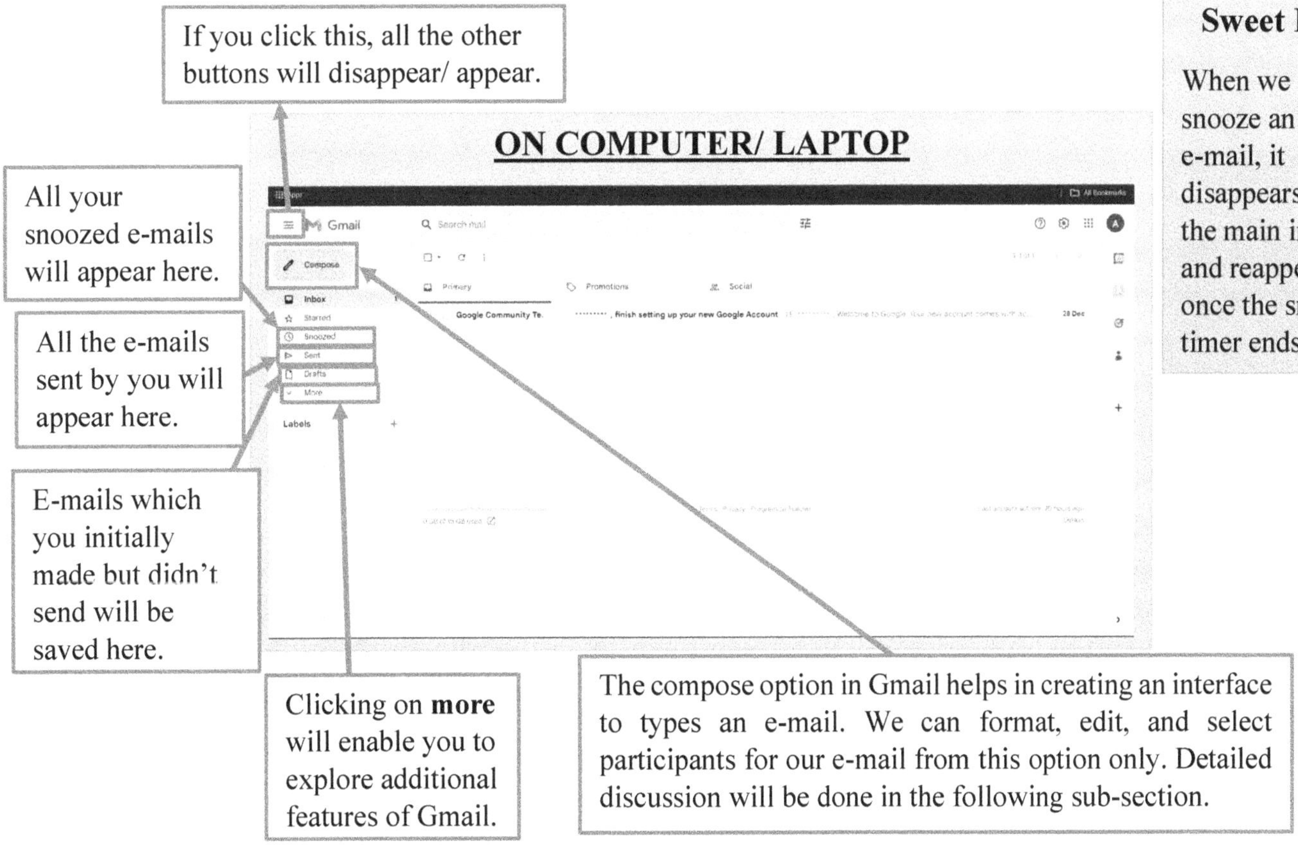

ON COMPUTER/ LAPTOP
You can search your mail by entering the subject/ sender/ content/ using filter.
Anyone who sends you e-mail will appear here.
You can star mark important e-mails and can read them whenever required.
All the personal and important e-mails are stored here.
E-mails related to promotional ads appear here.
E-mails from your social media platforms are displayed here.
You can see your account and personal details here. Your photo can also be added to your account profile photo.
All the Google based applications are stored here.
Gmail
Compose
Inbox
Primary
Promotions
Social

ON COMPUTER/ LAPTOP
If you click this, all the other buttons will disappear/ appear.
All your snoozed e-mails will appear here.
All the e-mails sent by you will appear here.
E-mails which you initially made but didn't send will be saved here.
Clicking on **more** will enable you to explore additional features of Gmail.
The compose option in Gmail helps in creating an interface to types an e-mail. We can format, edit, and select participants for our e-mail from this option only. Detailed discussion will be done in the following sub-section.
Gmail
Compose
Inbox
Primary
Promotions
Social
Labels

Sweet Bite

When we snooze an e-mail, it disappears from the main inbox and reappears once the snooze timer ends.

ON COMPUTER/ LAPTOP

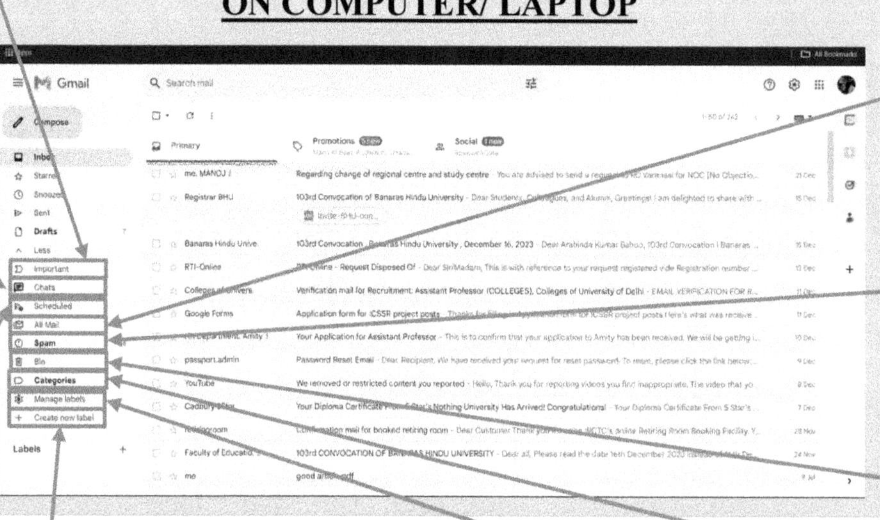

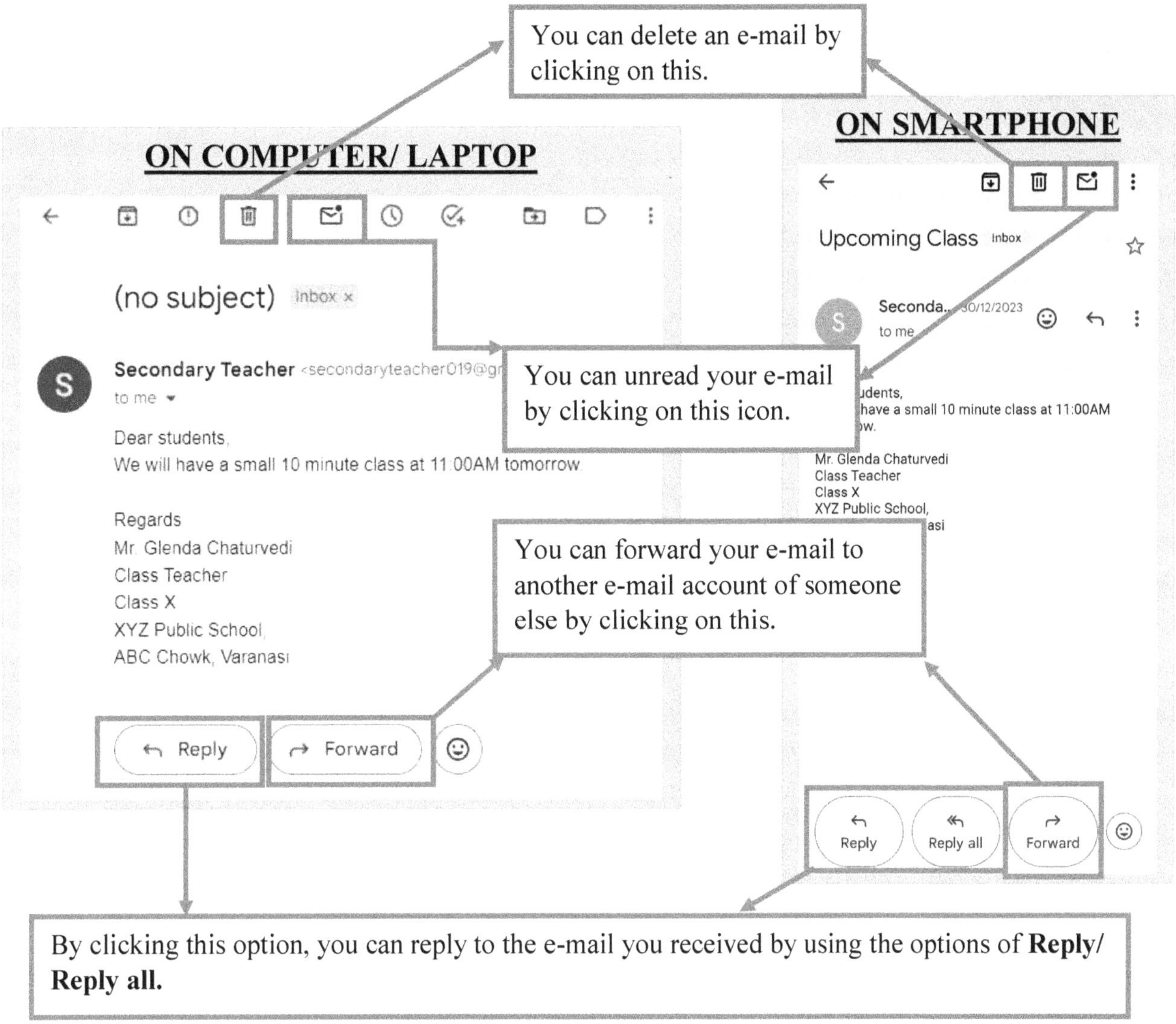

You can delete an e-mail by clicking on this.

ON SMARTPHONE

ON COMPUTER/ LAPTOP

Upcoming Class Inbox

(no subject) Inbox x

Seconda... 30/12/2023
to me

Secondary Teacher <secondaryteacher019@gr
to me

You can unread your e-mail by clicking on this icon.

Dear students,
We will have a small 10 minute class at 11:00AM tomorrow.

...dents,
...have a small 10 minute class at 11:00AM
...w.

Regards
Mr. Glenda Chaturvedi
Class Teacher
Class X
XYZ Public School,
ABC Chowk, Varanasi

Mr. Glenda Chaturvedi
Class Teacher
Class X
XYZ Public School,
...asi

You can forward your e-mail to another e-mail account of someone else by clicking on this.

Reply   Forward

Reply   Reply all   Forward

By clicking this option, you can reply to the e-mail you received by using the options of **Reply/ Reply all.**

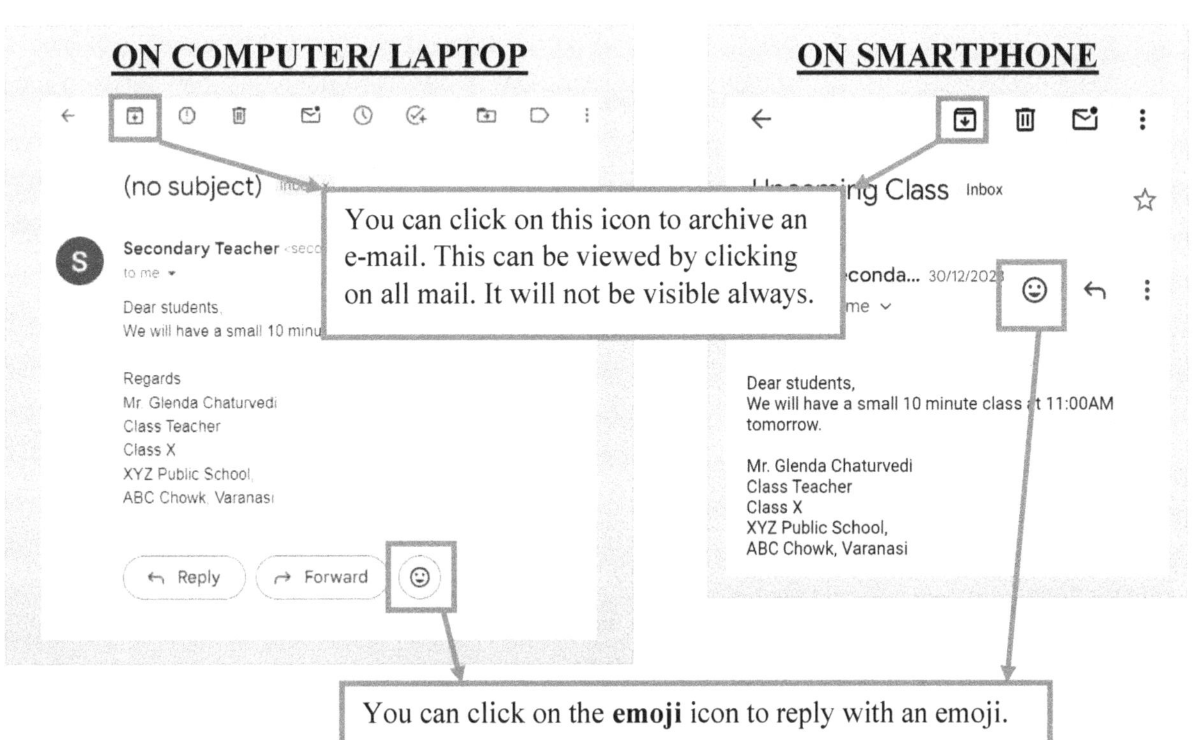

You can click on the **emoji** icon to reply with an emoji.

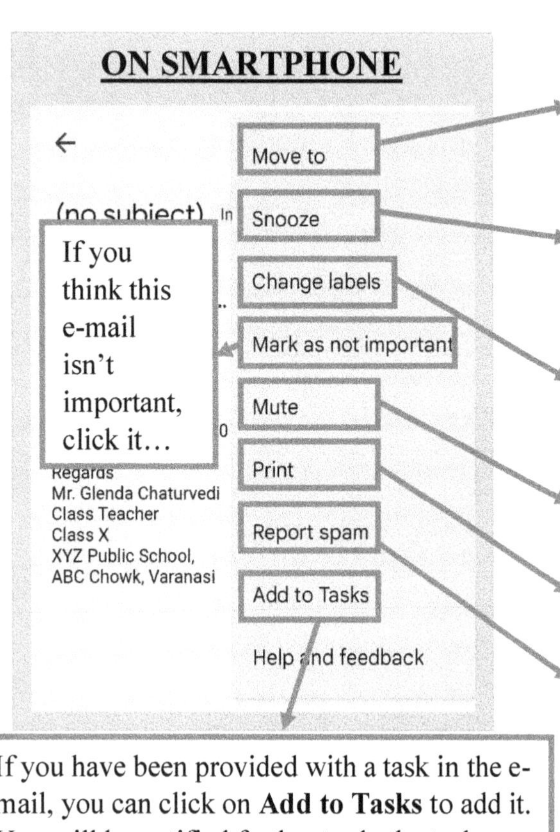

In this option, you can move the received e-mail from one label to another. For example, the e-mail from primary section to promotion or social or vice-versa.

You can snooze the received e-mail. This means the e-mail will again reappear at your selected time.

You can change the label. For example, you have created a new label of **Class X,** you can change the label from Inbox to Class X.

In the mute option, any further e-mails from this e-mail ID will not be notified to you.

You can print your e-mail from this option.

This option enables you to move any e-mail from this account to Spam folder.

If you have been provided with a task in the e-mail, you can click on **Add to Tasks** to add it. You will be notified further to do the task.

ON SMARTPHONE

By clicking the three dots just beside the sender's name, you can see the following options.

You can select reply all button from this also to reply to the received e-mail.

You can forward your e-mail to someone else using this option as well.

You can star mark an e-mail if you think it to be necessary from this.

You can translate the e-mail in language to your desired language.

You can print your e-mail from this.

Once you open an e-mail, it is marked as read. If you still want to keep it unread, click on this.

ON COMPUTER/ LAPTOP

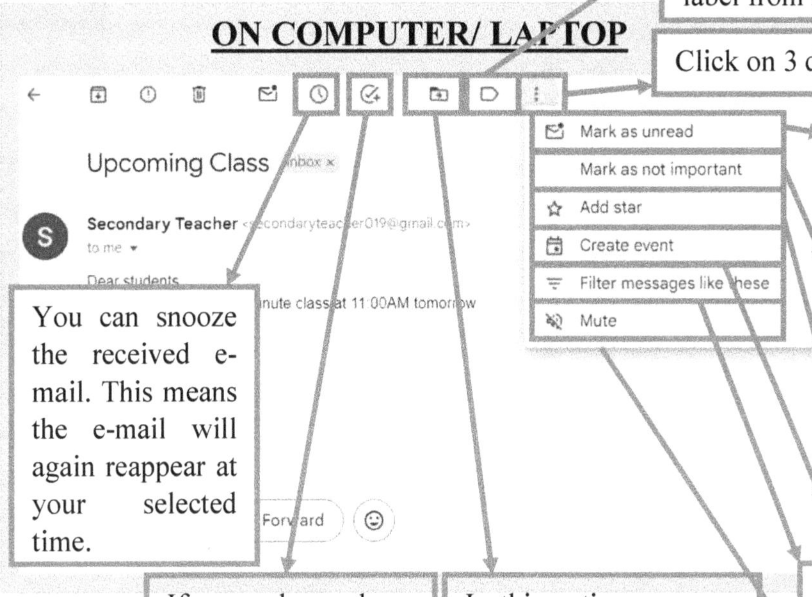

You can change the label. For example, you have created a new label of **Class X,** you can change the label from Inbox to Class X.

Click on 3 dots for more options.

Once you open an e-mail, it is marked as read. If you still want to keep it unread, click on this.

If you think this e-mail isn't important, click it…

You can star mark an e-mail if you think it to be necessary from this.

You can create an event with the other user using this for a task.

You can filter your message here.

You can snooze the received e-mail. This means the e-mail will again reappear at your selected time.

If you have been provided with a task in the e-mail, you can click on **this icon** to add it. You will be notified further to do the task.

In this option, you can move the received e-mail from one label to another. For example, the e-mail from primary section to promotion or social or vice-versa.

In the mute option, any further e-mails from this e-mail ID will not be notified to you.

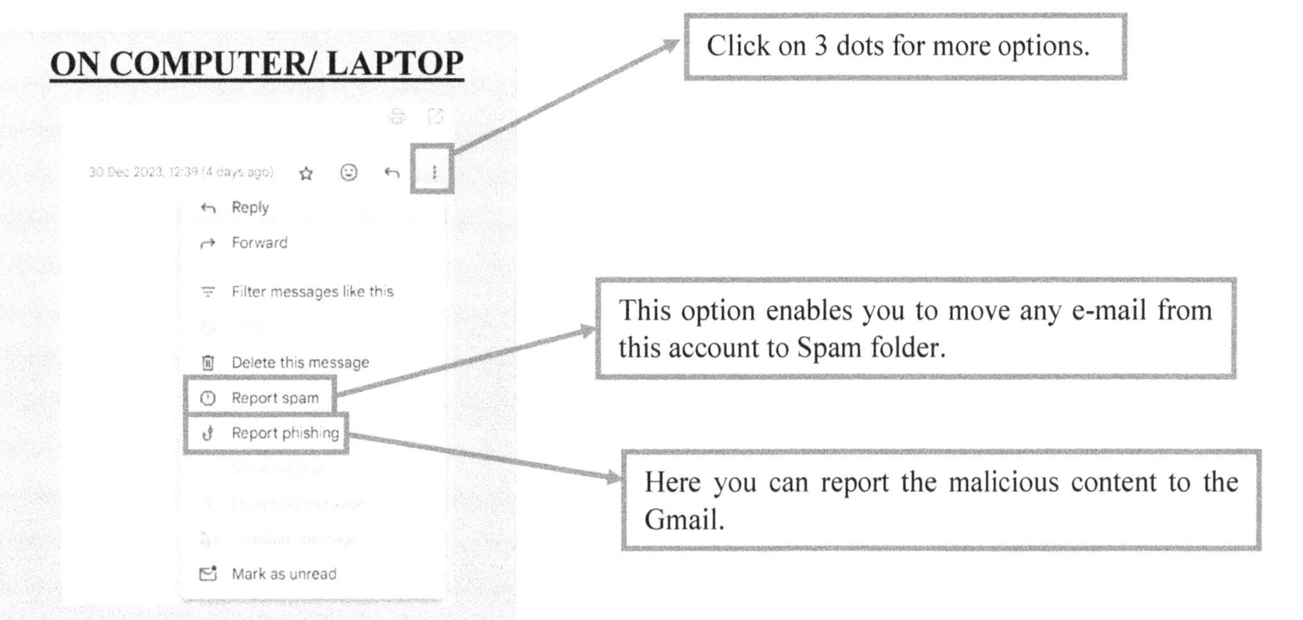

ON COMPUTER/ LAPTOP

Click on 3 dots for more options.

This option enables you to move any e-mail from this account to Spam folder.

Here you can report the malicious content to the Gmail.

1) What is the purpose of translate button?

(a) Revisiting the e-mail

(b) Removing the e-mail

(c) Changing the language of the e-mail

(d) Filtering the e-mail as per our interest

2) When we archive an e-mail, where can we see them?

(a) Spam

(b) Bin

(c) Draft

(d) All Mails

3) E-mails kept in bin are stored for how many days?

(a) 90

(b) 60

(c) 30

(d) 120

4) Snooze option in Gmail can be compared to which of the following?

(a) Scanner

(b) Alarm Clock

(c) Digital board

(d) Analogue watch

5) What is the purpose of compose button?

(a) Drafting an e-mail

(b) Verifying sender's identity

(c) Reporting e-mail to phishing

(d) Informing colleagues that I am writing an e-mail.

4) What is the purpose of Schedule option?

....

....

....

1.5. COMPOSING AND DRAFTING E-MAIL

We have already discussed on how to create an e-mail ID using Gmail and the different features of an e-mail account. Click on the link provided & get information on how to do all these stuffs.

How to compose and draft e-mails?

1.6. ADVANCED FEATURES OF E-MAIL

By this time, we have learned some of the basic details of e-mail so that we can use e-mail effectively in our everyday lives. Aspects like, sending e-mails, receiving e-mails, composing, and drafting e-mails have been discussed in the previous section of this module.

What if we don't want to let the receiver see the e-mail for a specific period? What if we want to see the image directly on the e-mail without downloading it? What if we want to put a password on our e-mail to make it more secure? What if we want to add signature in our e-mail?

These are possible in e-mails but sadly only on laptops/ desktops. Smartphones don't have such features as of now except the confidential mode. Now let's see how can we do these?

Inserting Emoji:

Click here: How to insert emoji?

Inserting Photo:

Click here: How to insert photo?

Enabling Confidential Mode:

Click here: How to enable confidential mode?

Setting Expiry:

Click here: How to set expiry?

Require Passcode:

Click here: How to enable require passcode?

Inserting Signature:

Click here: How to insert signature?

1.7. CREATION OF E-MAIL (OTHER THAN GMAIL):

Click the video below and follow the detailed guidelines provided to you with desired steps.

1. **Outlook**

2. **Hotmail**

How to create a hotmail account?

3. **Yahoo**

How to create a yahoo e-mail account?

LET'S CHECK OUR PROGRESS:

1. Develop an e-mail ID using the extension of @outlook.com.
2. Send a typed e-mail regarding the workshop report to yourself keeping workshop coordinator as cc along with your signature and a passcode.
3. Describe your experience on the difficulties faced by you while creating a Google account using this link.
4. Fill this form to check your understanding on e-mail management.

REFERENCES

Gmail: Private and secure email at no cost | Google Workspace. (n.d.). https://www.google.com/intl/en_in/gmail/about/

How to Google. (2020, June 29). *How to create Google Account* [Video]. YouTube. https://www.youtube.com/watch?v=1uJ1TxklS2Y

Learning Education. (2020, April 17). *Electronic mail | Use of email in education |* [Video]. YouTube. https://www.youtube.com/watch?v=LnUmSfKMFeg

Microsoft 365. (2020, April 23). *How to set up your work email with Outlook* [Video]. YouTube. https://www.youtube.com/watch?v=hyYvKzNJNek

The Lady from UNCLE. (2022, June 23). *How to create a NON-Gmail email Google Account | 2022* [Video]. YouTube. https://www.youtube.com/watch?v=3qPOEDyxpcU

GOOGLE DRIVE

2. MODULE CONTENTS:

2.1. Module Objectives
2.2. Introduction
2.3. Initiation Google Drive
2.4. Introduction to Google Drive interface
2.5. Management of Google Drive
2.6. Advanced Features of Google Drive

2.1. MODULE OBJECTIVES:

The teachers and teacher educators will be able to:

- Conceptualize the idea of Google Drive.
- Create and upload files using Google Drive.
- Share and locate files in Google Drive.
- Use advanced features of Google Drive.

2.2. INTRODUCTION:

Google Drive is a free service from Google that allows individuals to store files online and access them anywhere using the cloud. Google Drive also gives users access to free web-based applications for creating documents, spreadsheets, presentations and more. One of the most widely used cloud storage services available right now is Google Drive. Give the benefits of storing your files online some thought if you haven't used a cloud-based storage service like Google Drive before. Drive solves the need to email or save files to a USB drive by enabling file access from any computer with an Internet connection. Additionally, sharing files with others is made much simpler by Drive.

As Google Drive is an application developed by Google, we need to have an active Google account i.e., a @gmail.com account. As we have already created Google account. We will now directly jump to the use and operation of Google drive.

2.3. INITIATION OF GOOGLE DRIVE:

Google Drive is an important tool for management of all your files online. Google drive can be accessed using https://drive.google.com on the search engine installed on your computer/ laptop. However, in case of smartphones, click on the Google Drive icon on your screen interface.

2.4. INTRODUCTION TO GOOGLE DRIVE INTERFACE:

Let's now see how the Google drive homepage looks like along with information on additional button and options available in Google drive and their functionality.

<u>INTRODUCTION TO DRIVE INTERFACE</u>

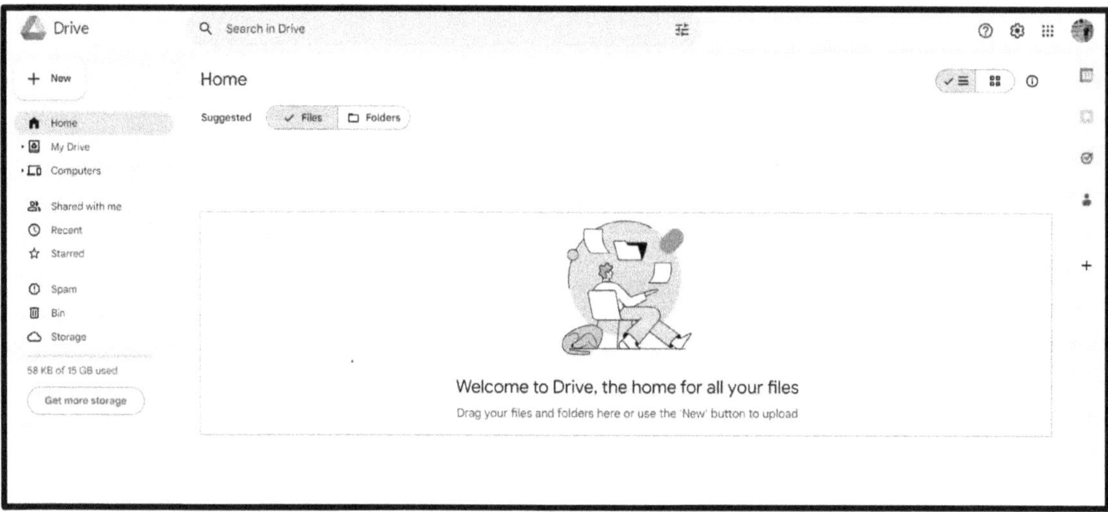

✛- To create/ upload new files/ folders.

⌂- To view all the activities done by you in the files/ folders.

▣- To view all the files and folders uploaded to Drive or shared to you.

⌐- To view all the files and folders of your device synced with the Google Drive.

⧑- To view shared files and folders only.

◷- To view recent activities done in your Google Drive.

☆- To view starred files/ folders.

◉- To view spam folders/ files.

🗑- To view the deleted files/ folders.

2.5. MANAGEMENT OF GOOGLE DRIVE:

Management of Google drive becomes one of the hectic tasks for a teacher educator/ teacher in the day-to-day life. Let's see how to use Google Drive in a stepwise manner.

1. <u>Creating files on Google Drive:</u>

Just like any other offline file manager, like the one in your smartphone, Google drive is useful in creating files of different formats as per our convenience. Google drive doesn't just store the files; it also allows to create, share, and manage documents with its own productivity apps. It has certain applications that helps in creating files. These include:

- Google Docs- It is useful in composing letters, creating learning materials, and other text-based files (It is quite like Microsoft Word).

- Slides- It is useful in preparing presentations and slideshows (It is quite like Microsoft PowerPoint).

- 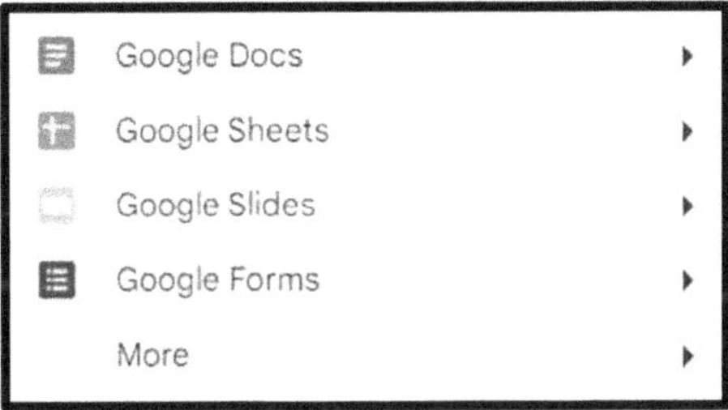 Spreadsheets- It is useful in making all kinds of tables and calculations in a sheet and organizing & storing information (It is quite like Microsoft Excel).

- Forms- It is useful in assessment and data collection purposes by the teachers and teacher educators.

- Meet- It is useful in video conferencing and conducting online classes.

- Keep- It is useful in saving different important information and taking notes of it.

- Drawings- It is useful in creating different simple vector graphics or diagrams (It is quite like Paint in computers).

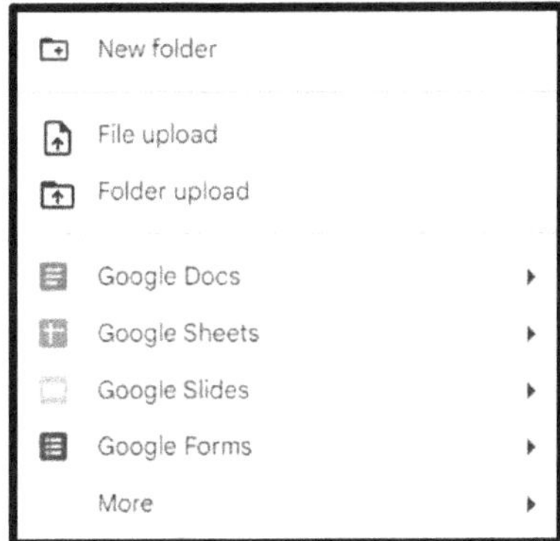

2. <u>Uploading files and folders:</u>

It is easy to upload files from computer to Google drive. If we use the Google Chrome web browser, we can even upload entire folders. This can be done using the **NEW** button.

On Computer/ Laptop.

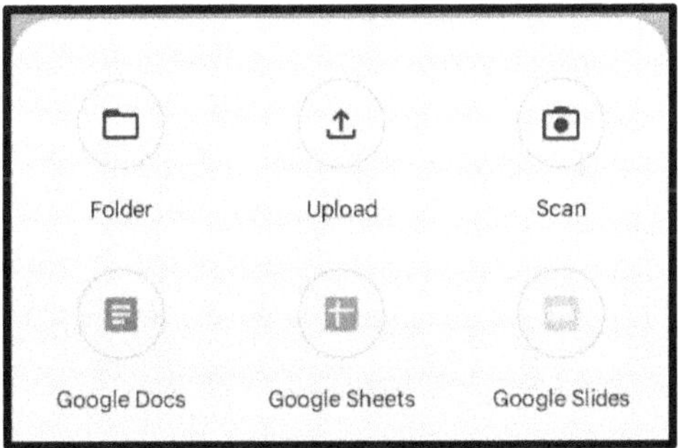

On Smartphones.

3. **Organizing files:**

   Once we start adding files to Google drive, we can use **folders** to help organize and group them. Folders in Google Drive work just like the one in the computer/ smartphone.

4. **Searching files:**

   Searching lets us look for specific files using words contained within the file or file name. To do this, locate the **search bar**, then enter the word, or file name you are looking for. A list of suggested searches and files will appear as we type. Simply click on a file to open it directly from the search results. We can also press the **Enter** key to see a full list of search results.

Q   Search in Drive

You can also watch the video below to know more:

2.6.   LET'S CHECK OUR PROGRESS

1. Check the Google form below and attempt the questions:

   https://forms.gle/JyKGz2VjZFaW98RH6

2. Create a folder on this workshop and share with the workshop coordinator as editor.
3. Write your reflections from this module through an in-built application of Google Drive and share with the workshop coordinator.

2.7.   FURTHER SUGGESTIONS AND REFERECES:

K. S. (2020, December 2). *How to use Google Drive - Tutorial for Beginners*. YouTube.

   https://www.youtube.com/watch?v=gdrxAoqfvbA

How to use Google Drive - Computer - Google Drive Help. (n.d.).

   https://support.google.com/drive/answer/2424384?hl=en&co=GENIE.Platform%3DDDesktop

GOOGLE CLASSROOM

3. MODULE CONTENTS:

3.1. MODULE OBJECTIVES

The teachers and teacher educators will be able to;

- Conceptualize the idea of Google classroom.
- Create a Google classroom and add their students in the classroom.
- Use Google classroom to share materials, provide assignments, evaluate, and interact with the students.
- Use advanced features of Google classroom.

3.2. INTRODUCTION

Have you ever wondered; can we even teach outside classroom? No, no, we are not talking about classes held beneath the tree or home tuitions. Is it online classes then? Well, though we can take classes online using different video conferencing apps. But can we read and evaluate student's assignments in online classes, yeah, we can…. But for this, we have a specialized application developed by Google Inc. named Google classroom.

What's a Google classroom? Is it a physical classroom developed by Google with all modern technologies?

Google classroom is an online application, that allows the students to receive learning materials, ask questions to the teachers, interact with the classmates, and also helps teachers share learning materials, create quizzes, create assignments, evaluate the assignments, conduct tests etc.

It is a free blended learning platform developed by Google for educational institutions that aims to simplify creating, distributing, and grading assignments. The primary purpose of Google Classroom is to streamline the process of sharing files between teachers and students.

Need of Google Classroom:

The teaching-learning scenario is continuously changing from being rhetoric and conventional to technological web-based classroom. It helps teachers connect with the students virtually without a direct verbal interaction. The teachers can monitor students using this software.

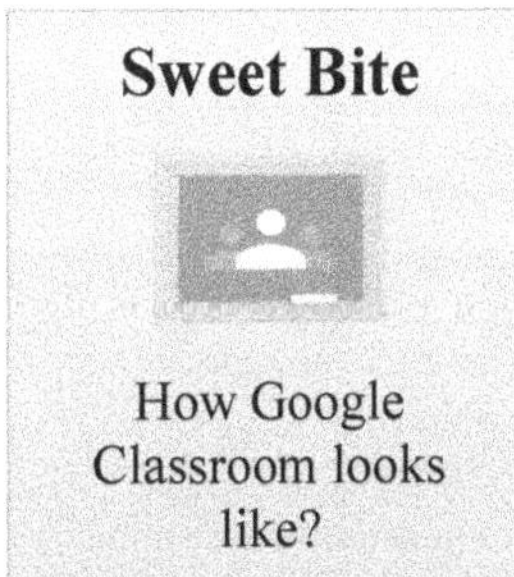

Sweet Bite

How Google Classroom looks like?

3.3.   CREATION OF A GOOGLE CLASSROOM ACCOUNT

A Google classroom is a default application of Google Inc. Hence, you don't need to activate/ create a Google classroom account in order to use. A Gmail account is sufficient for this. In the application "Google Classroom" we are supposed to create different classrooms as per our requirement, like classroom of Class 10 Science subject, Class 9 Mathematics subject.

Let's now see how we can login into Google classroom first by clicking here.

How to create a Google classroom account?

3.4.   INTRODUCTION TO GOOGLE CLASSROOM INTERFACE

The next step in this process is understanding the Google classroom interface. Let's see what different buttons in the interface are supposed to do.

Home- In the home button, you can see the different classes joined/ created by you during the course of time. Along with this, upcoming tasks, either to be completed by the students or you will also appear here.

Calendar- In the calendar button, you can see your upcoming events from Google classroom. For example, you have given students of class 9 a deadline to complete assignment by 11:00PM on 01/011/2024, the same will be visible in your calendar as well. If you joined a classroom, where a trainer posted a quiz to be attempted by midnight, this will also be visible in Google calendar.

Archive classes- In this option, you can archive the classes you no longer need/ want to get updates from. If you are a teacher and archive a classroom, it will be archived only from your side, if you want to get it disabled from the students' side also, you will have to delete the Google classroom.

Settings- In the settings option, you can change your Google account profile and also modify your Google classroom interface.

Create class- In the create class button you can create a classroom for your desired class and section and add the students either by sending them e-mail or messaging them through any other medium or by providing them Google classroom's passcode.

Join class- Here you can join a classroom by entering the classroom's passcode. The create and join option can also be done from the "+" icon available in the top right corner.

Let's now see pictorial representation:

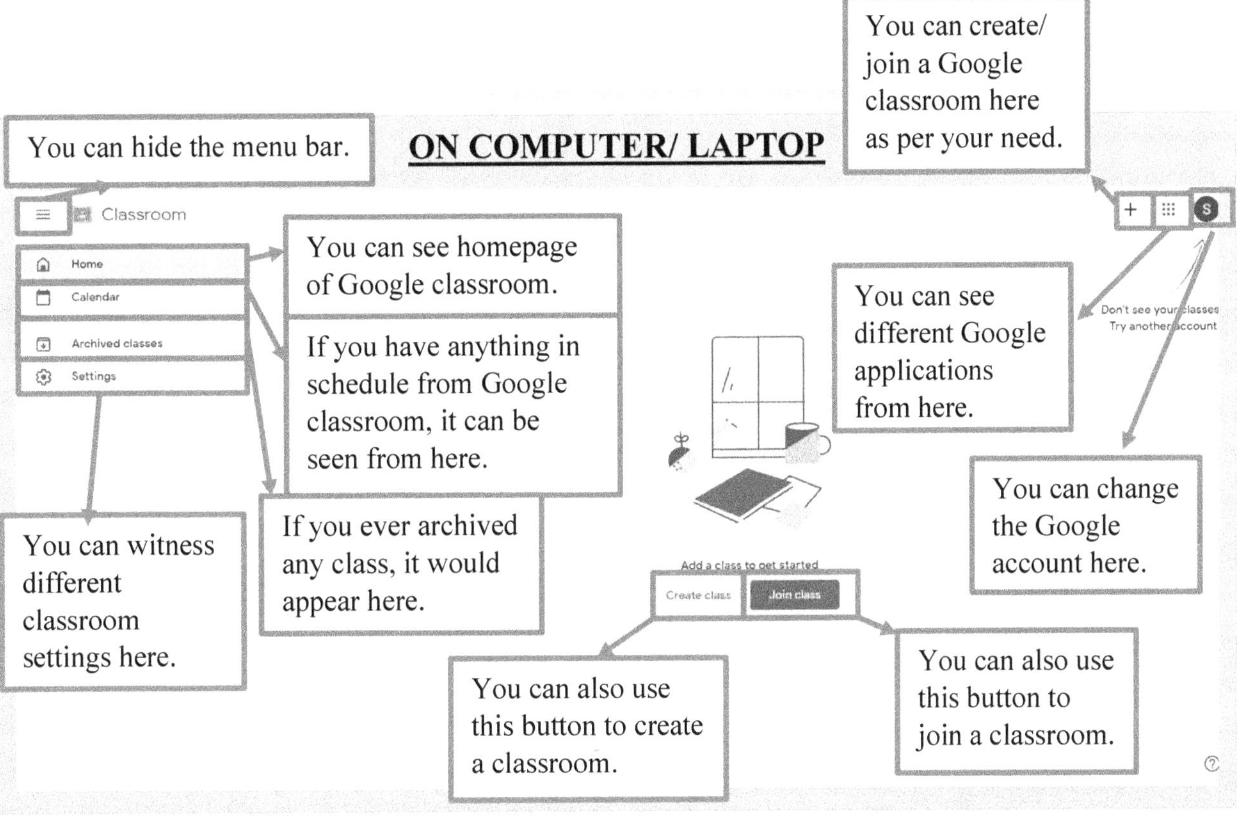

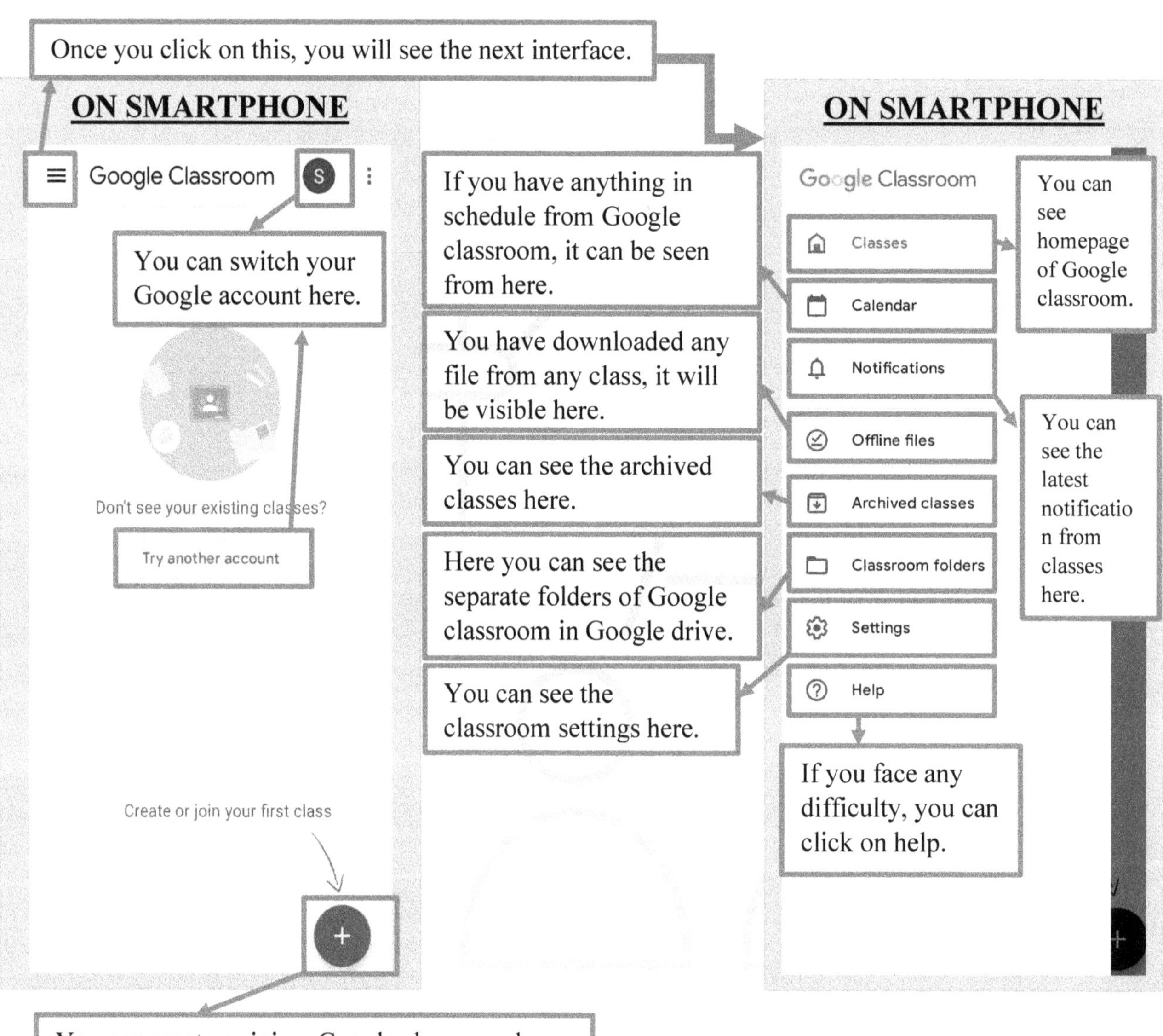

Once you click on this, you will see the next interface.
ON SMARTPHONE
Google Classroom
You can switch your Google account here.
Don't see your existing classes?
Try another account
Create or join your first class
You can create or join a Google classroom here.
If you have anything in schedule from Google classroom, it can be seen from here.
You have downloaded any file from any class, it will be visible here.
You can see the archived classes here.
Here you can see the separate folders of Google classroom in Google drive.
You can see the classroom settings here.
ON SMARTPHONE
Google Classroom
Classes
Calendar
Notifications
Offline files
Archived classes
Classroom folders
Settings
Help
You can see homepage of Google classroom.
You can see the latest notification from classes here.
If you face any difficulty, you can click on help.

3.5. CREATION OF A GOOGLE CLASSROOM

Since we have already discussed how to create a Google classroom account, how the Google classroom interface looks like, let's now further our discussion on how we can create a Google classroom through Computer/ Laptop/ Smartphone.

The stepwise discussion can be done using the link below.

A step-by-step guide to create Google classroom

3.6. MANAGEMENT OF GOOGLE CLASSROOM

After creating your classroom, you will be redirected to your new classroom page. Here, you will see the different classroom options, along with the option to add your students into the classroom (either by code or by sending them e-mails, if you know their e-mail ID).

Let's now see what the different buttons are available in the classroom page.

Teaching- The teaching option gets activated only after you create at least one classroom.

To review- The **'to review'** is meant for reviewing the works, tasks or materials shared by you to your students.

Stream- In the stream option, you can see all the activities in that specific classroom.

Classwork- You can post your learning materials, assignments, tasks here. Along with it you can also check student's activities on assigned tasks from here.

People- In this section, you will have information of the students who joined the class. You can also join students further or remove the students joined the class.

Marks- Here, you can evaluate the students on the basis of their performance on assigned tasks.

Calendar icon- This calendar icon is different from the main calendar icon in the homepage of classroom. In this calendar icon, you will get information of your activities of that specific class.

Drive icon- The drive icon inside a specific classroom opens directly into that classroom folder in Google drive. The files uploaded by you, or the students can be seen from this icon.

Classroom settings- The classroom settings option inside a specific class gives you access to edit the permissions and usability for the members of the class. It will be seen in the class creator's account only.

Class code- Here the class code of a specific class created by you will be visible. You can share/ send the class code to your students to let them join in the class.

Upcoming- Teachers have plenty of stuffs to keep in mind. In such a scenario, google classroom keeps you informed about upcoming activities that you have scheduled on classroom using Google calendar.

Announce something to your class- In this section, you can directly interact with the students like any other messaging or chatting platforms, but here the conversation will be in the group. Students can ask their questions here, post their queries, discuss with the teachers or classmates, teachers can supply supplementary materials here as well.

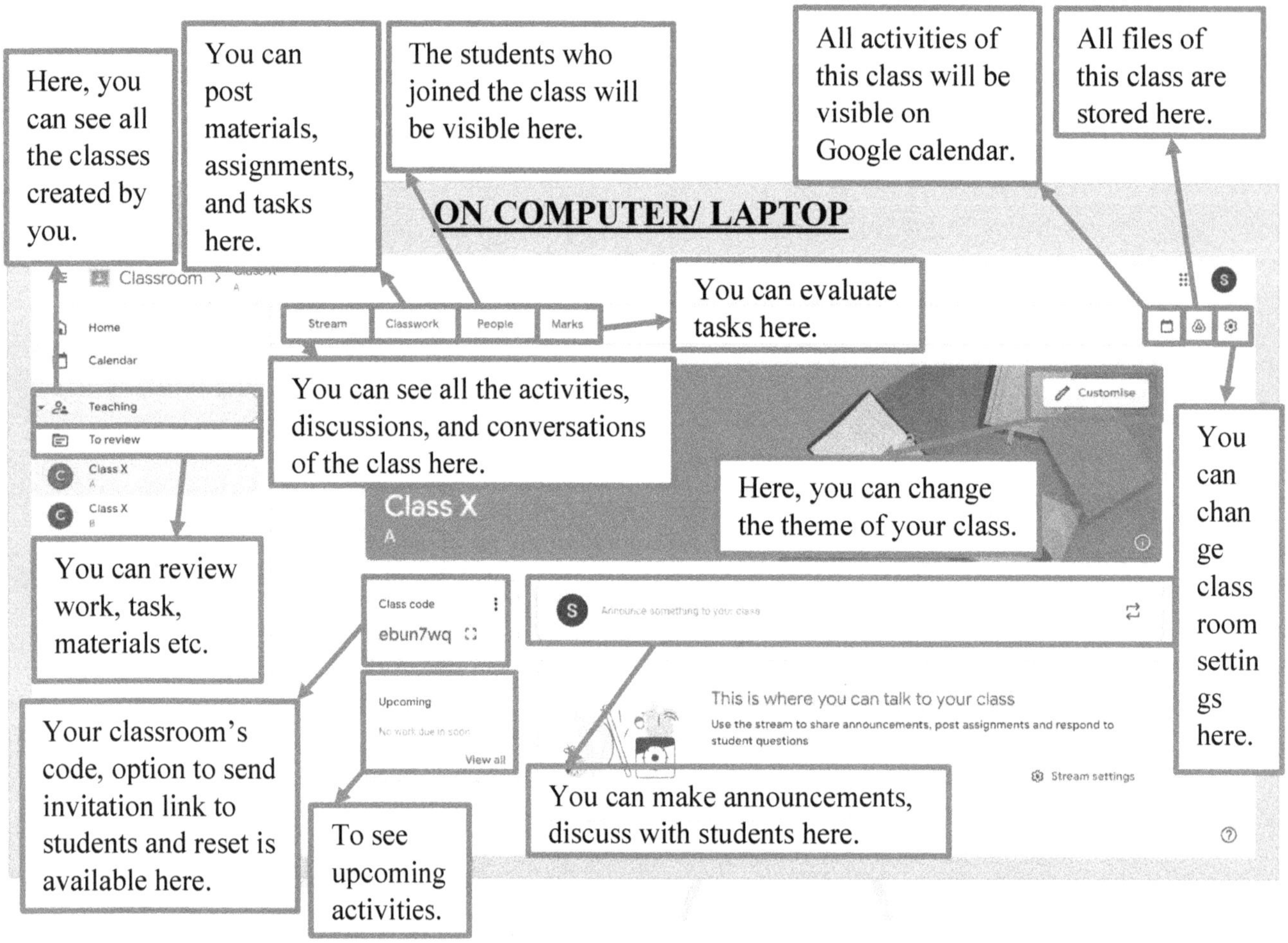

Here, you can see all the classes created by you.

You can post materials, assignments, and tasks here.

The students who joined the class will be visible here.

All activities of this class will be visible on Google calendar.

All files of this class are stored here.

ON COMPUTER/ LAPTOP

You can evaluate tasks here.

You can see all the activities, discussions, and conversations of the class here.

Here, you can change the theme of your class.

You can change classroom settings here.

You can review work, task, materials etc.

Your classroom's code, option to send invitation link to students and reset is available here.

To see upcoming activities.

You can make announcements, discuss with students here.

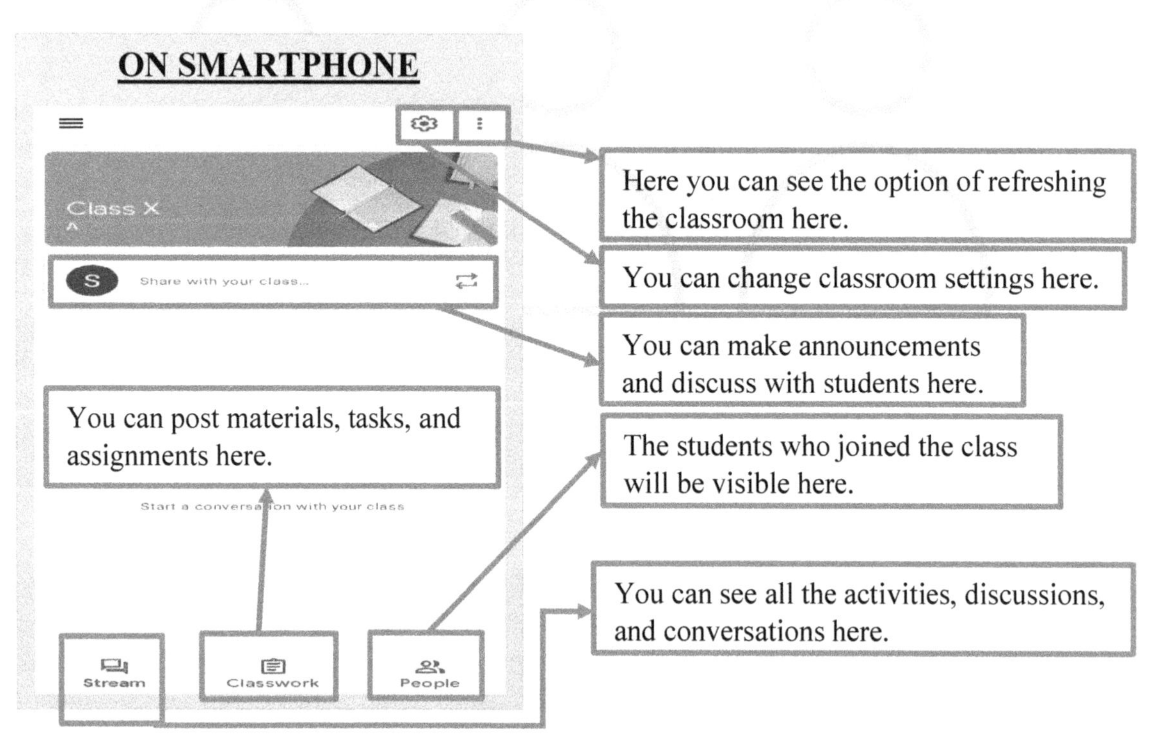

ON SMARTPHONE

Here you can see the option of refreshing the classroom here.

You can change classroom settings here.

You can make announcements and discuss with students here.

The students who joined the class will be visible here.

You can post materials, tasks, and assignments here.

You can see all the activities, discussions, and conversations here.

Since, we have already seen the interface of Google classroom application as well as specific classroom. Let's now see how we can add students to the classroom, how we can share materials, assignments, make a deadline, evaluate etc. in the classroom.

How to add students/ teachers into Google classroom?

As we have already created a google classroom, let's now see how we can add students or teachers into the classroom.

We can add students basically by 3 different methods:

1. By sending them invitation link to their registered e-mail address.
   Below two options can only be done using laptop/ computer:
2. By sending them invitation link through any other messaging platform.
3. By providing them classroom code so they can join directly.

These 3 steps are dealt in detail in the link provided below.

How to add students in the classroom

How to share materials/ assignment on classroom?

CLICK HERE TO KNOW MORE ON HOW TO ADD MATERIALS IN GOOGLE CLASSROOM

3.7.   ADVANCED FEATURES OF GOOGLE CLASSROOM

There are a few advanced features that Google classroom offers to the students and the teachers to make the learning more fruitful. The additional features of Google classroom include,

i.   Grading the students.
     Click here to know more about this feature.
ii. E-mailing students within the classroom
     Click here to know more about this feature.

3.8.   WHAT WE UNDERSTOOD:

Since we have already concluded our discussions on Google classroom, let's now see what we understood:

1. If we want to create a quiz using Google classroom, which external website is mandatory?
   a. Google Docs
   b. Google Forms
   c. Microsoft Excel
   d. Google Slides
2. What cannot be done using Google classroom?
   a. Assignment
   b. Grading
   c. Material
   d. Ranking

3. Can we move topics in the Google classroom? (Yes/ No)
4. What is the function of archive classes option in Google classroom?
5. Other than people option, where can we send private messages to students?
6. How can we remove a student from the Google classroom?
7. What are the different interfaces in Google classroom where students can comment and converse with their batchmates or teachers?
8. How calendar is useful in Google classroom? Explain.
9. After creating a classroom, elaborate how you will help the students in joining the classroom by filling the following form: https://forms.gle/ajHgDRJJXyLZxCj39
10. Elaborate on creation of a quiz along with timer using Google classroom.

3.9.   FURTHER READINGS AND SUGGESTIONS:

Adding to this module, you can also refer to the following external websites:

Get started with Classroom for teachers - Android - Classroom Help. (n.d.).
https://support.google.com/edu/classroom/answer/9582854?hl=en&co=GENIE.Platform%3DAndroid

National Institute of Technology, Meghalaya (n.d.). *Instruction for the students to join and work with Google classroom.*
https://www.nitm.ac.in/uploads/9ea1c0db467b2029e99399e4b3b81d12.pdf

Rainbow, C. (2020, 24 March). *Supporting every teacher: Using Google classroom to share work with students.* Cambridge University Press & Assessment.
https://www.cambridge.org/elt/blog/2020/03/24/using-google-classroom-to-share-work-with-students/

United Federation of Teachers (n.d.). *Google classroom tutorials.*
https://www.uft.org/teaching/classroom-resources/online-teaching/google-classroom-tutorials

University of Delhi (n.d.). *Google Classroom User Manual.*
https://www.du.ac.in/uploads/Google_Classroom_UserGuide.pdf

GOOGLE MEET

4. MODULE CONTENTS:

4.1. Module Objectives
4.2. Introduction
4.3. Creation of a meeting link
4.4. Management of meet
4.5. Advanced features of meet

4.1. MODULE OBJECTIVES:

The teachers and teacher educators will be able to:

- Conceptualize the idea of Google meet.
- Create and conduct online meetings and classes.
- Invite, share, manage and present in online meetings and classes.
- Use additional features of Google meet to make fruitful meetings and classes.

4.2. INTRODUCTION:

Google developed a platform for video conferences called Google Meet. It is intended for online collaboration, remote communication, and virtual meetings. Google Meet is a platform that facilitates real-time discussions, presentations, and collaboration by enabling users to host and participate in video meetings with friends, clients, or coworkers. It has different functions that helps in providing real-time experience in virtual mode, a few include:

1. Video Conferencing: We can conduct video conferences with participants present from all around the globe at a time.
2. Scheduling Meetings: We can set a specific timer in our Meet invite link which will be activated only at the appropriate timing and students/ colleagues can join them.
3. Scheduling using Google calendar: The meetings can also be scheduled using Google calendar, where Google calendar will notify you at the appropriate time.

In short, we can also summarize by stating that Google meet is an upgraded version of any video calling application with extended number of participations at a time.

4.3. CREATION OF A MEETING:

SMARTPHONE

Go to Gmail/ Google Meet Application → Click on New Meeting → Select the option as per your convenience from 1. Get a meeting link to share/ 2. Start an instant meeting/ 3. Schedule in Google calendar → Share the link to your intended contacts through different mediums.

COMPUTER/ LAPTOP

Go to Google Meet website/ use https://meet.google.com link → Click on New Meeting → Select the option as per your convenience from 1. Get a meeting link to share/ 2. Start an instant meeting/ 3. Schedule in Google calendar → Share the link to your intended contacts through different mediums.

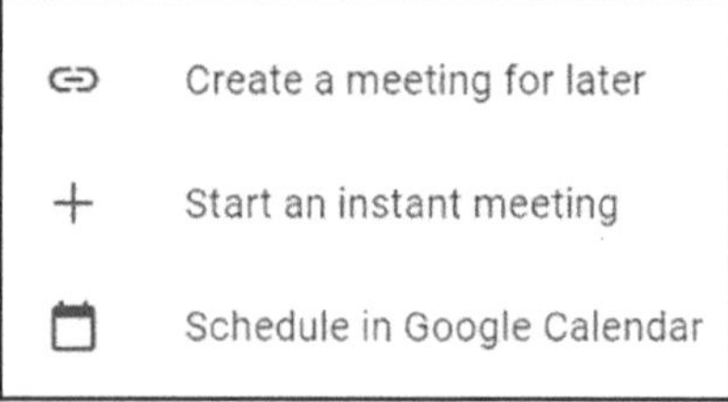

These 3 options in the Google meet lets you start a meeting as per your convenience. In the 1st option, you can create a meeting link now and use it later. The 2nd option enables you to start a meeting immediately. The last option helps you schedule your meeting in Google calendar which will be later helpful in scheduling meetings on any time schedule.

4.3. MANAGEMENT OF MEET:

The interface of Google meet in Computer/ Laptop and Smartphone varies significantly. We will now look into the interface of the Google meet.

: To mute or unmute sound.

: To show/ hide your video during meeting.

: To show subtitles of the ongoing meeting (Applicable in English only)

: To react to the class using different emojis.

: To share your screen for presentation.

: To quit/ exit the meeting.   : To turn on bike mode.

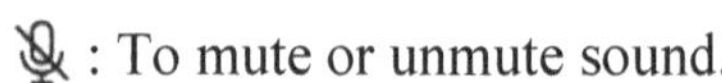

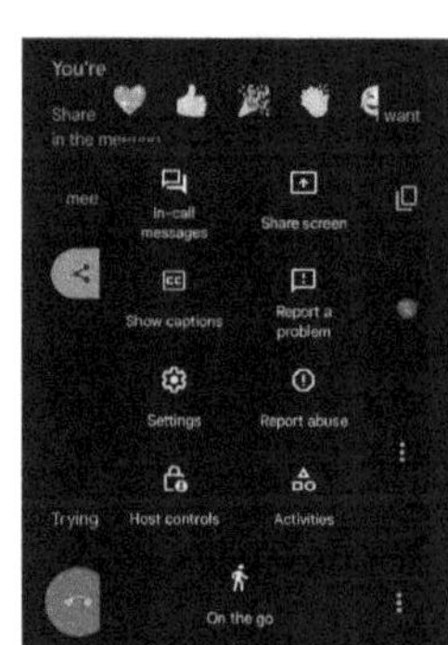

: To raise hand in case of any grievance/ confusion. It will be notified to other members.

: To know further about the meeting/ Google meet.   : To see the activities of the meeting.

: To view the participants who joined the meeting.   : To control the activities by the host.

: To start conversations/ view the conversation in the meeting.

We can share our different activities in our Google meet. It may include PowerPoint presentations, worksheets, PDFs etc. To do this, the step is as follows:

Click on ⬆/ Share screen option → Select the tab you want to display/ Close the meet application and open the file in your smartphone → Click on share.

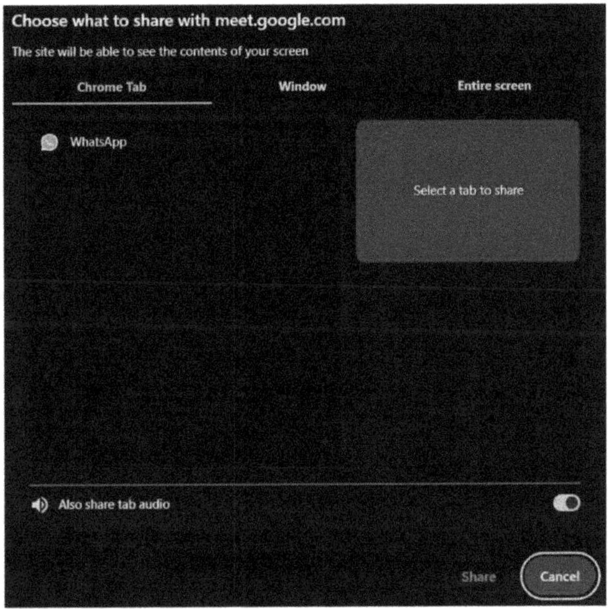

You can now present your intended document in the meeting/ class.

Though this option is only available in Computer/ laptop, but this is an option that makes the class/ meeting effective through direct interaction in terms of blackboard conversation. Here, you can write like any other class while teaching.

Click on Whiteboard (Open a jam) → Click on "Start a new whiteboard" → Click on meet icon → Click on bring the call here/ Present this tab.

The features mentioned above are some of the basic functions done by Google meet. Let's see some additional features, that we can use to make the online meeting/ class more conducive.

1. Pinning Profile:
   This option enables you to pin any of the participants in your home screen. The steps are as follows:
   - On laptop/ computer: Clicking on ⊓ for the account you want to pin.
   - On smartphone: Clicking on ⋮ of that profile and click on pin.
2. Muting/ Removing participants:
   This option enables you to either mute the participant remove him/ her from the meeting in case of special cases/ disturbances.
   - On laptop/ computer: Click on 🎤 of that respective participant to mute and click on ⊖ of that respective participant to remove from the meeting.
   - On smartphone: Click on ⋮ of that respective participant and click on mute/ remove as per the requirement.
3. Switching Camera:
   This option is only available in smartphones on whether you want to use front or back camera during the meeting.

Besides, you can use the following icons to get a more detailed description on how to use Meet.

1. Click on the Google Drive link and upload screenshot of your Google meet interface.
   https://drive.google.com/drive/folders/1GdqDd8R7AHXAlOtcWUwjP8ca3GWxaYQV?usp=sharing
2. Click on the icon and check your understanding on Google meet. 🗒
3. Create a Google meet link and share to us using the e-mail ID option.

4.7.   REFERENCES & FURTHER SUGGESTIONS:

Google Workspace. (2023a, April 21). *Google Meet: Start a video conference* [Video]. YouTube. https://youtube.com/playlist?list=PLU8ezI8GYqs4a5NQpjBU-xgZvp2uVPd8E&si=xzkdt9hgZylmTpaM

IIT Hyderabad (n.d.). *Simple instructions for Google meet.* https://people.iith.ac.in/anomalies19/Instructions_for_Google_Meet.pdf

University of Kashmir (n.d.). *Google meet guide.* https://uok.edu.in/download/googlemeet.pdf

GOOGLE WORKSPACE

5. MODULE CONTENTS:

5.1. Module Objectives
5.2. Introduction to Google workspace
5.3. Creation & Management of Google Docs
5.4. Creation & Management of Google Slides
5.5. Creation & Management of Google Spreadsheet
5.6. Using shortcut keys to make the work faster.

5.1. MODULE OBJECTIVES

The teachers and teacher educators will be able to;

- Create Google docs, Google slides & Google sheets.
- Use Google features to enhance teaching learning process.
- Use shortcut keys in the Google workspace.

5.2. INTRODUCTION

Do you remember the session of Google drive? There we discussed something similar to these names. But wait aren't they a part of Google drive? Why do we need another session on it?

Let's answer this first. Google drive is storage space provided by Google. Here we create, store, and manage our data of different extensions (like .pptx, .docx, .xlsx, .pdf, .mp4 etc.) at one place. We can access such things using Google drive **as well**. But these are not a part of Google drive but can be created through Google drive too. Google workspace can't be discussed single-handedly in the Google drive. For which, this module is created. We will now focus on what Google workspace are discussed here and why are they required?

These Google workspaces are used as substitute to other software for creating documents like our typed form of document, presentation making, creating sheets for record maintenance etc. But if we have other workspace, why should we use Google's application? Here is why.

The Google workspace can be created only with a valid e-mail address. Whereas, in other cases, you are supposed to create one more account. These are easily accessible and editable both from smartphones and tablets and computers too. Other than this, we don't need to purchase any subscription to use it and we can also share the document with live editing option by other users.

The Google workspace included in this module are:

1. **Google Docs-** The Google Docs is used for creating word files and documents.
2. **Google Slides-** The Google Slides is used to create presentations which can be used in classes for make the class interactive.
3. **Google Sheets-** The Google Sheets is used to create, edit, and share spreadsheets to maintain records of the daily activities and other information.
4. **Google Forms-** The Google Forms is used to create questionnaires, rating scales etc. generally for our assessment purposes (it will be dealt in next module).

We will now see how we can open these applications. You can visit them using the link provided below.

1. **Google Docs-** https://docs.google.com
2. **Google Slides-** https://slides.google.com
3. **Google Sheets-** https://sheets.google.com

The video below will help you in understanding the different functions of the three applications along with a brief introduction of the interface of these applications.

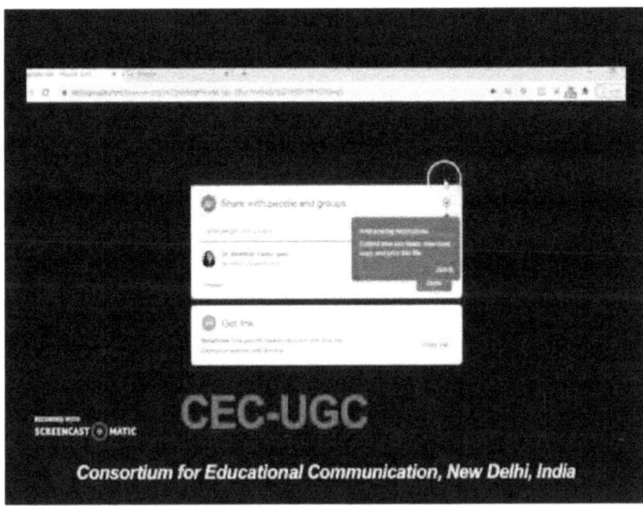

If you don't have a computer/ laptop, click on the below link to know on how to use Google workspace using smartphones.

5.2.   HOW TO USE GOOGLE DOCS

1. Creating a new document:

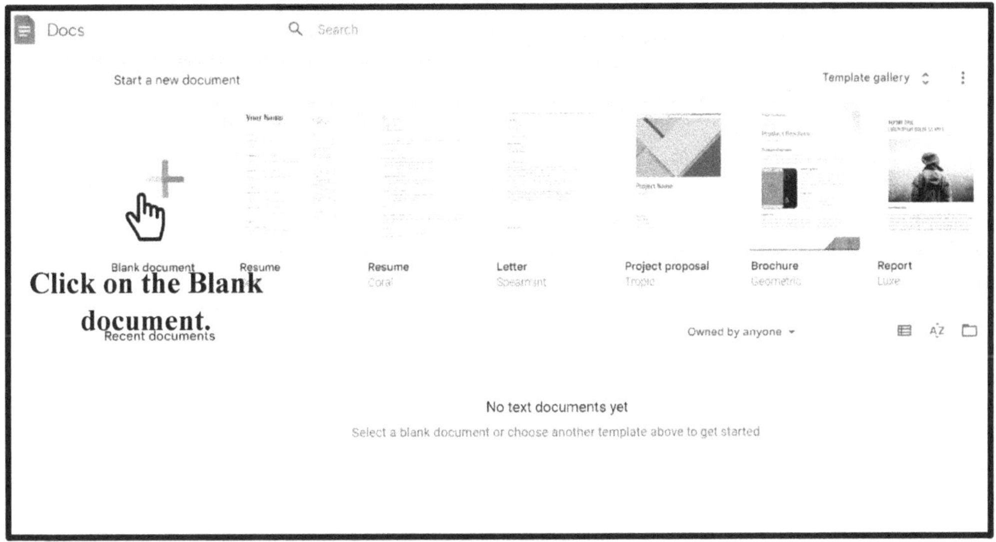

2. Editing, Drafting and Designing a document:

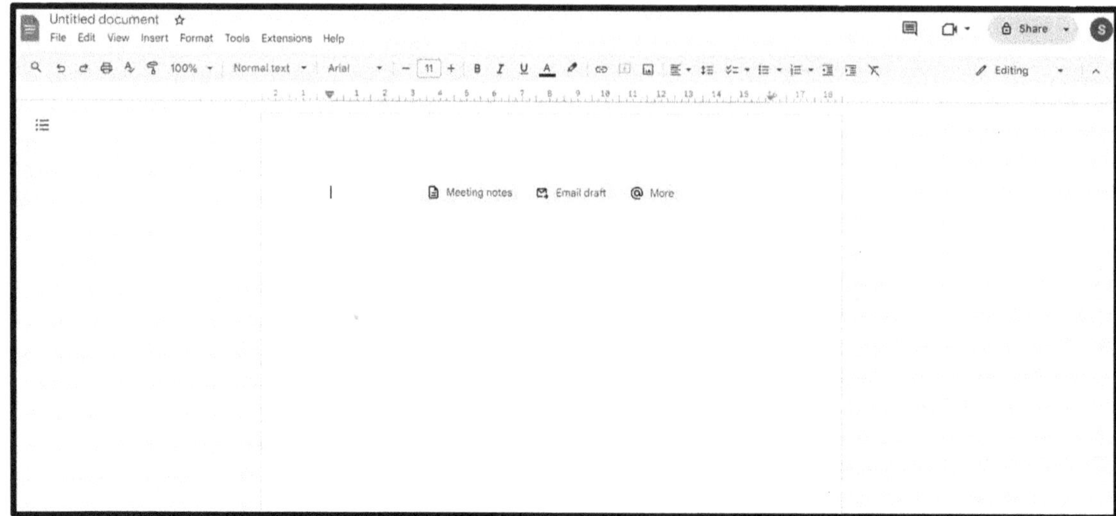

You will see a blank page like this where you can type your text, edit, design, and format them from the available options like **edit, view, insert, format, tools, extensions** etc.

Besides, if you want to download the file or save it to your drive, you can do this using the **file** option along with the options of e-mailing document, sharing it, language setting, page setup etc. available in the same button.

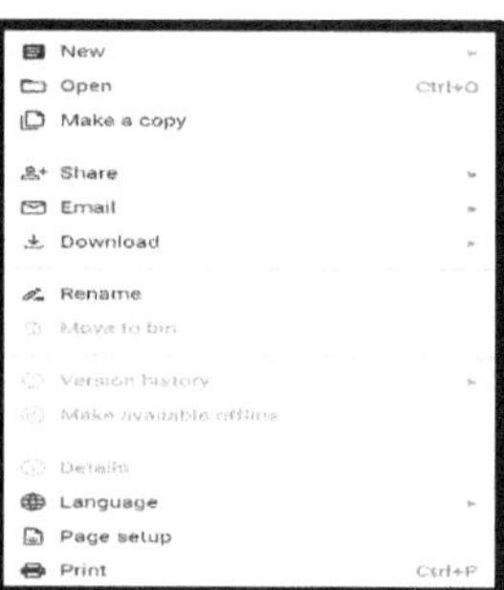

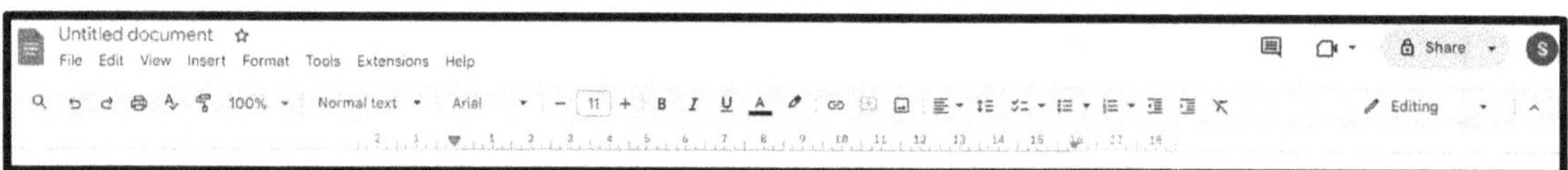

🔍- To search within a file.   ↺- To undo a task.   ↻- To redo a task.   🖨 To print the document.

🗸 - To check grammar and spelling.   🎨- To add colour in the background.

Normal text- To modify the paragraph style. **Arial** and **-11+ -** To change the font style & size.

B- To bold text.   *I-* To italicize text.   <u>U</u>- To underline text.   <u>A</u>- To add font colour.

✏- To highlight the text.   🔗- To insert link.   ⊞- To add comment in the text.

🖼- To add image in the text.   ≣- To manage alignment.   ⇕≣- To manage paragraph spacing.

☑ ▾- To manage checklist.   ≔ ▾ ≔ ▾- To add bullets in the text.   ✕- To clear formatting.

3. Sharing a document:

You can click on the **share** button available on the top right corner of the page. By sharing the document, you and the receiver can edit it live at the same moment from different devices and different locations.

Besides this, you can also enable others to comment on your document using the message option and the document can also be shared in live conferences using the meet icon, however, it is only functional for conferences done using Google meet only.

These are the basic features of Google docs what you need to know about. However, there are much more complex options here, which you should explore by yourself by using the video provided below as a guide.

Click on the below video to know more about Google Docs.

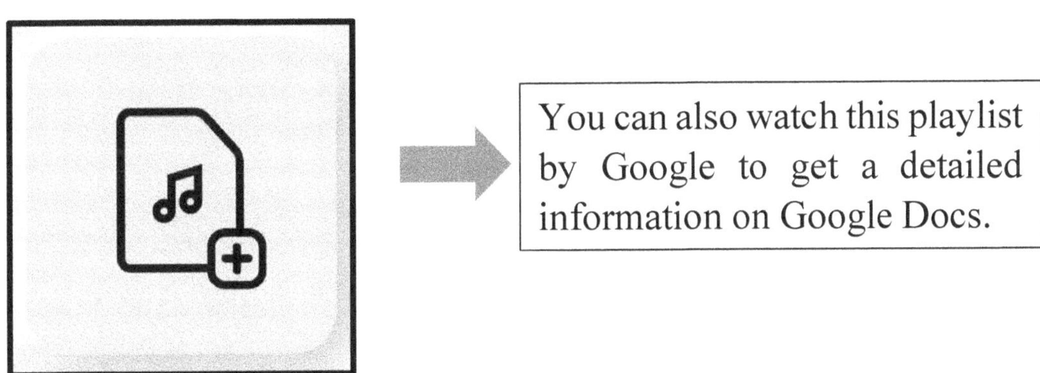

You can also watch this playlist by Google to get a detailed information on Google Docs.

What did we learn?

1. Share two documents created in Google Docs. One should be shared directly from the application and the other should be shared using Google Drive.
2. Click on the link below and attempt the questions:

   https://forms.gle/o2hDPPpdQHnRU89aA

5.3. HOW TO USE GOOGLE SLIDES

1. Creating a new document:

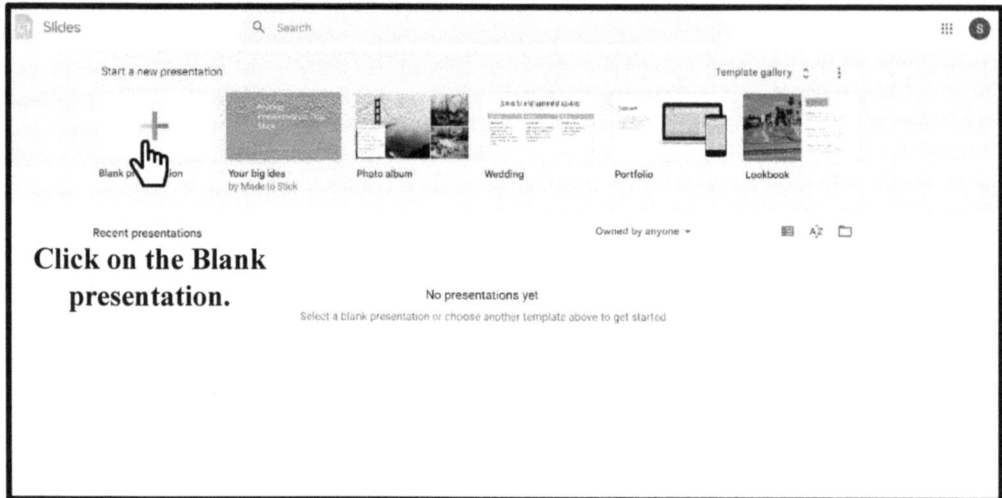

Click on the Blank presentation.

2. Editing, drafting, and designing a slide:

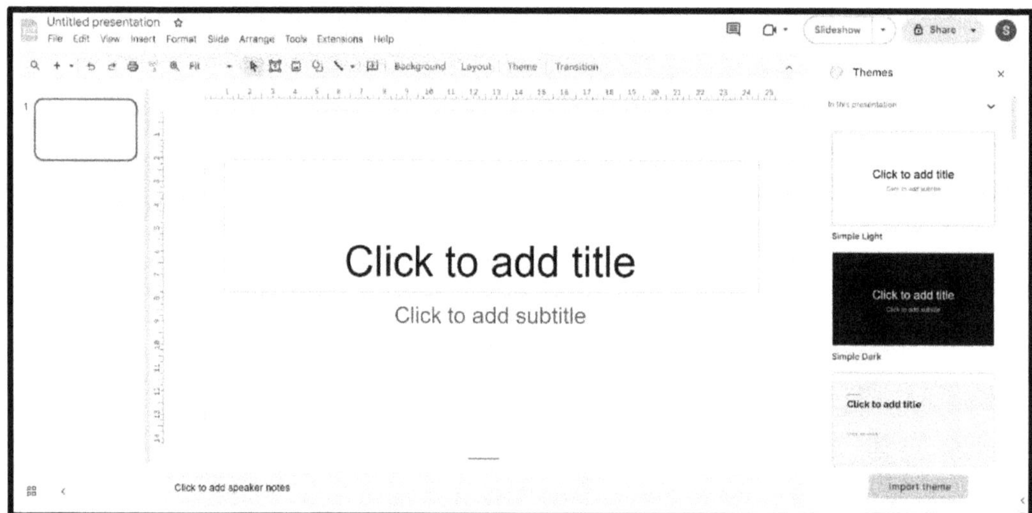

You will see a blank page like this where you can type your text, edit, design, and format them from the available options like **file, edit, view, insert, format, arrange, tools, extensions** etc.

Besides, if you want to add/ manage slides, you can do this using the **slide** option along with the options of adding new slide, duplicating slide, deleting slide, skipping slide, moving slide, changing background, applying layout, transition, editing theme, changing theme etc.

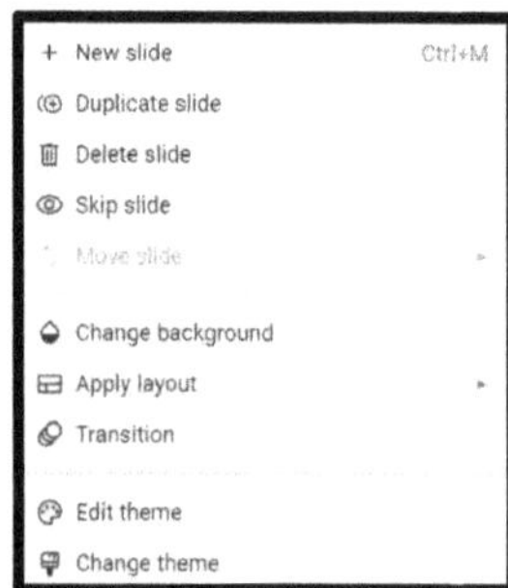

$\mathcal{Q}$- To search within a file. $+$- To add slide. $\supset$ - To undo a task. $\complement$ - To redo a task.

$\boxminus$- To print the slide. $\overline{\mathbb{L}}$- To add colour in the background. $\mathcal{Q}$- To zoom into slide.

Fit- To manage slide zoom. $\mathbb{k}$ - To select slide. $\boxed{\text{T}}$- To add a textbox in the slide.

$\mathcal{O}$- To add shape. $\diagdown$- To add lines. $\boxplus$- To add comments.

Background- To change background.   **Layout**- To apply layout.   **Theme**- To change theme.

Transition- To add transition effects to your slides.

If you add a textbox in the slide, the same options as that of Google Docs will appear.

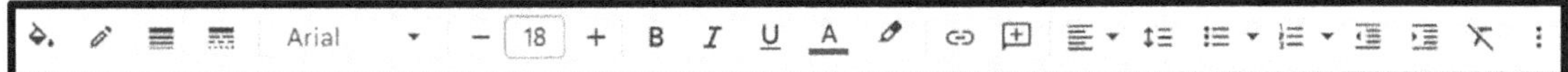

3. Starting Slideshow:
You can click on the **video call or Slideshow** button available on the top right corner of the page. Slide can be presented directly or through the Google meet link.

Besides this, you can also see version history from $\mathbb{O}$ icon. Version history include all the changes made in the slides along with the timestamp. $\boxed{\text{E}}$ icon enables to see comment history on your slides. The sharing option is similar to that of Google Docs.

These are the basic features of Google Slides what you need to know about. However, there are much more complex options here, which you should explore by yourself by using the video provided below as a guide.

Click on the below videos to know more about Google Slides.

> **What did we learn?**
> 1. Share two documents created in Google Slides. One should be shared directly from the application and the other should be shared using Google Drive.
> 2. Present and record a slideshow and share it using a Google drive link.
> 3. Click on the link below and attempt the questions:
> https://forms.gle/gHUFWT679oysv7NN7

1. Creating a new document:

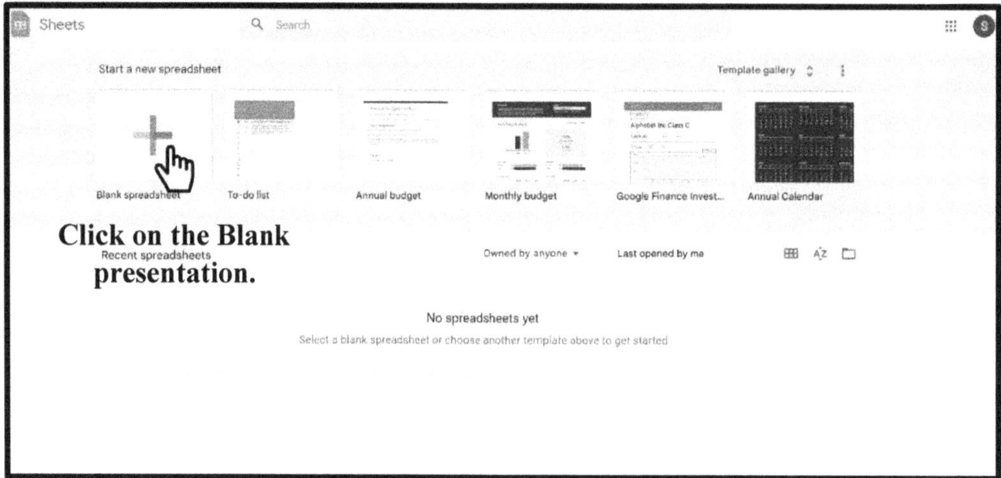

Click on the Blank presentation.

2. Editing, Drafting and Designing a document:

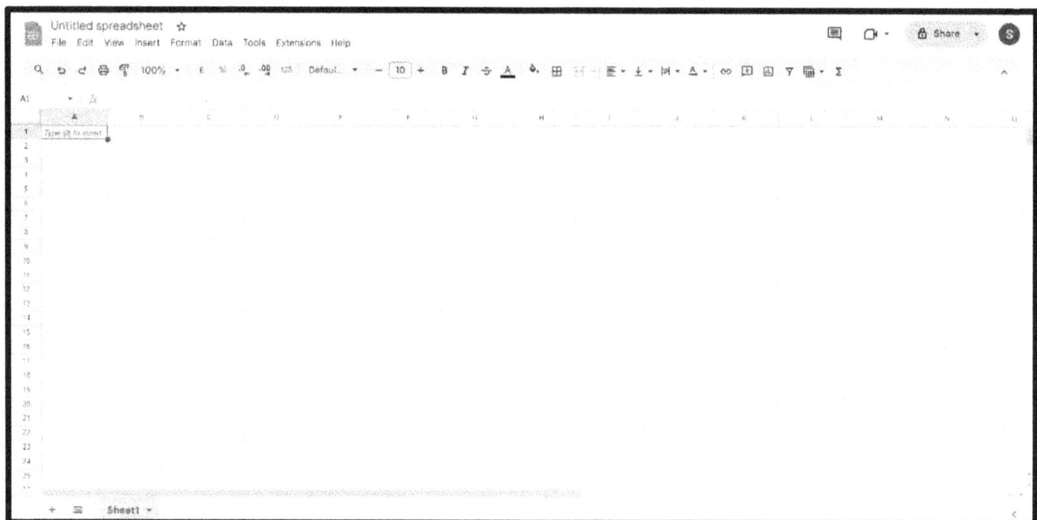

You will see a blank sheet like this where you can type your text, edit, design, and format them from the available options like **file, edit, view, insert, format, tools, extensions** etc.

Besides, if you want to manage information entered in the sheets, you can do this using the **data** option along with the options of sorting sheet, sorting range, creating filter, viewing filter, adding slicer, protecting sheet & range, named function, randomising range, viewing column statistics, validating data, cleaning-up data, splitting text to column, extracting data, using data connector etc.

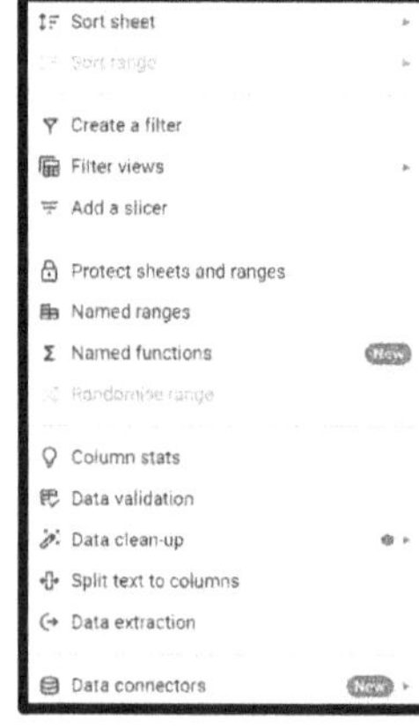

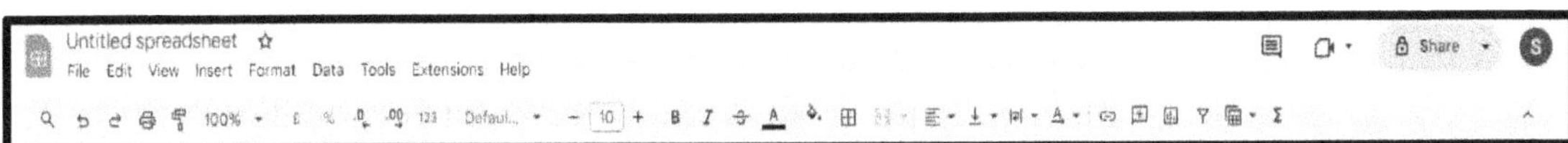

$\mathcal{Q}$- To search within a file. $\supset$- To undo a task. $\mathcal{C}$- To redo a task.   🖶- To print the sheet.

🎨- To add colour in the background.   **100%**- To zoom into sheet.   **£**- Formatting as currency.

%- Formatting as percentage. $\cdot 0$- Decreasing decimal place. $\cdot 00$- Increasing decimal place.

123- To see more formatting options.   **Default** & **-10+**- To change font style/ size.

B- To bold.   *I*- To italicize.   ÷- To ~~strikethrough.~~   **A**- To add font colour.

🖉- To add text colour.   ⊞- To add border in cell.   ⧉- To merge cells.

≡- To manage horizontal alignment.   ⊥- To manage vertical alignment.   ⇥- To wrap text.

A- To rotate text.   🔗- To insert link.   ⊞- To add comment in the text.   📊- To insert chart.

𝖸- To create filter.   ⊞- To filter views.   **Σ**- To add functions like sum, average etc.

3. Sharing Sheets:

This is similar to the one done in Docs and Slides.

Click on the below video to know more about Google Sheets.

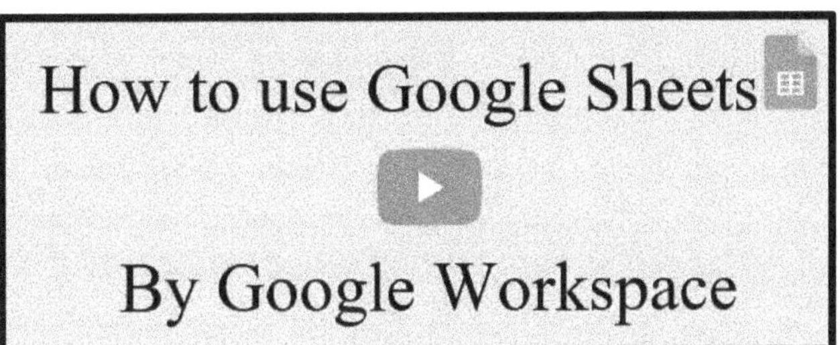

What did we learn?

1. Create a spreadsheet with 3 individuals as editor (excluding the workshop coordinator) and enter the provided data and carry out the required calculations and edits.
2. Click on the link below and attempt the questions:
   https://forms.gle/1tWQ6XPnucf68U3WA

5.5.   SHORTCUT KEYS:

The following shortcut keys are useful in making the work faster. These include:

ctrl+ A= Selecting everything in the file

ctrl+ B= To **bold**

ctrl+ C= To copy

ctrl+ D= To download

ctrl+ F= To find in the file

ctrl+ H= To replace a word/ document in the file.

ctrl+ I= To *italicize*

ctrl+ K= To insert hyperlink

ctrl+ N= To create new file

ctrl+ O= To open a file

ctrl+ P= To print

ctrl+ S= Save the file

ctrl+ U= <u>To underline</u>

ctrl+ V= To paste

ctrl+ W= To close the file

ctrl+ X= To cut

ctrl+ Y= To redo

ctrl+ Z= To undo

5.6.   LET'S CHECK OUR PROGRESS:

1. Create and associate Google Docs, Sheets and Slides in such a manner that each can be accessible from one link, Share the same using the following link:

2. The link below has a record of students marks in 3 subjects. Add their obtained marks using sheets formula and place it on a separate column. Prepare a chart-based presentation from the obtained score of the students using Google slides and export the chart into the Google Docs with your reflections. Share the 3 files with the workshop coordinator.

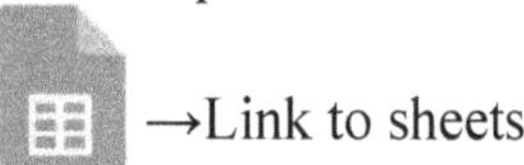 →Link to sheets.
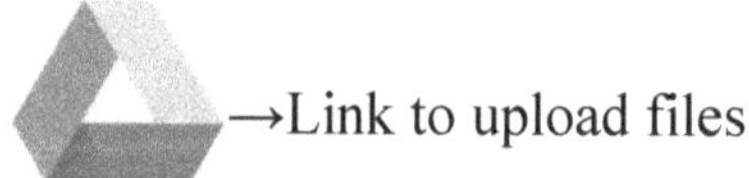 →Link to upload files.

5.7. REFERENCES AND FURTHER SUGGESTIONS:

Centre for Faculty and Support (n.d.). *Google Docs Tutorial.* San Jose State University.
    https://www.sjsu.edu/cfd/docs/Google%20Docs.pdf

Dube, R. (2020, 15th September). *How to use Google Docs: A Beginner's Guide.* Putnam
    County Public Library. https://pcpl21.org/wp-content/uploads/2020/09/How-To-Use-
    Google-Docs.pdf

Elmhurst Public Library (n.d.). *Google Docs, Sheets & Slides.*
    https://elmhurstpubliclibrary.org/lib/wp-
    content/uploads/GoogleDocs_Handout_072317sv.pdf

Pilani Atmanirbhar Resource Centre (n.d.). *Lesson 8: Google Slides Tutorial.*
    https://static1.squarespace.com/static/5e01f7481c79407e08d2cca0/t/5f4c03d30fd7671
    8433e578d/1598817270484/Lesson+8_+Google+Slides.docx.pdf

YouTube Links:

CEC. (2020, July 22). *Digital Tools for Education - G Suite* [Video]. YouTube.
    https://www.youtube.com/watch?v=1nyvWKOzLIc

Google Workspace. (2024, January 9). *Who needs a personal stylist when you have #DuetAI?*
    [Video]. YouTube. https://www.youtube.com/watch?v=OWrfJ8bSEKM

Google Workspace. (2023, December 20). *Google Sheets keeps all the sweet things you're
    doing for yourself.* ☑ *#Shorts* [Video]. YouTube.
    https://www.youtube.com/watch?v=YXlKDMcS9hQ

Google Workspace. (2020, March 6). *Copy selected slides in Google Slides* [Video].
    YouTube. https://www.youtube.com/watch?v=P5P-MIjiAUs

NCERT OFFICIAL. (2021, March 23). *Webinar on ICT Tools : "Create and Collaborate
    with Google Docs"* [Video]. YouTube.
    https://www.youtube.com/watch?v=bJ0pXUUmBBE

GOOGLE FORMS

6. MODULE CONTENTS:

6.1. MODULE OBJECTIVES

The teachers and teacher educators will be able to;

- Conceptualize the idea of Google Forms.
- Create Google Forms.
- Manage the Google Forms.
- Use advanced features of Google forms.

6.2. INTRODUCTION

Teachers in their day-to-day classroom use different assessment tools to check the progress of the students. These assessment techniques include opinionnaire, questionnaire, checklist etc. which we generally make in a rhetoric manner, i.e., by using pen and paper, and sometimes we get those sheets photocopied to reach large number of students. Adding to this, the summative assessments these days are conducted in the form of MCQs, where teacher uses a lot of time in evaluating the response sheets.

In this technologically advanced world, the assessment has turned much more easier using online assessment tools. Google Forms is a step-forward in this direction. But still, we find a huge gap in utility and applicability of this tool by the teachers and teacher educators in their day-to-day lives as most are still unaware of such facilities available to them at no additional cost. So, let's see what Google Forms is and how it is useful for us.

6.3. CREATION OF GOOGLE FORMS

Google Forms can be created by two methods:

1. By directly going to the portal https://docs.google.com/forms.

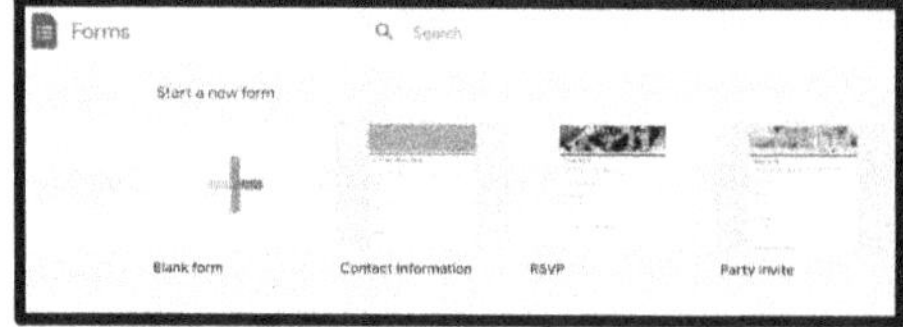

Choose from the available templates or click on Blank form/ + icon.

2. Through Google Spreadsheets.

Click on the **Tools** tab in spreadsheet and click on **Create a new form**.

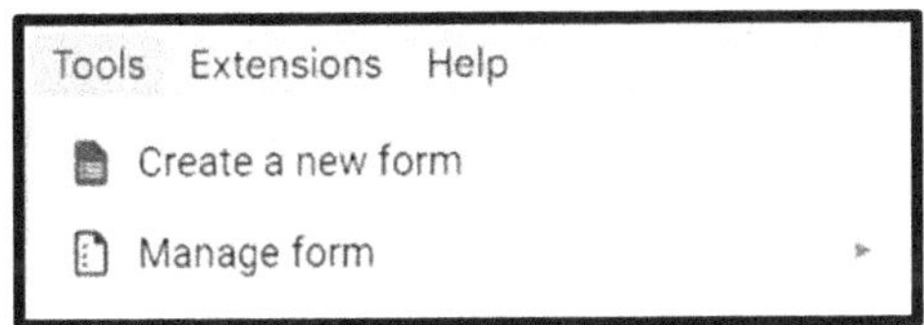

3. After you click on Blank forms/ Create a new form, an interface like this will appear on your screen.

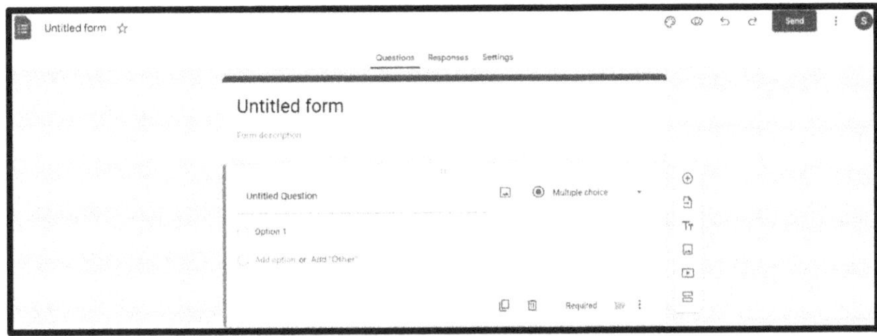

Here you can add title to your Google form, provide a description of your form along with other features like,

⊕- To modify the theme of your Google form.

👁- To preview your form.

Send- To share the Google form using different ways.

⟲- To undo the activity.

⟳- To redo the activity.

⋮- To view additional options.

Adding Questions in Google Forms:

- Click on the Untitled Question to type your questions. Based on the nature of the question you enter; Google Forms will automatically detect the kind and nature of questions and prepare the format of answer sheet. However, if you're not satisfied with

the detected format, you can change it from the dropdown available. You can click on the link below to view on adding different matters.

View More

- If you have more items to add, you can simply click on ⊕ to add more items. The newly added items will be in default option like a new one. However, if you want to keep the item's format intact, you can click on ⬜ to copy the same format.

- In case you have a Google form available, where the items you require to add are available then you can click on 🗗 icon to import them from the available Google form. Once you click on it, you will have options of available Google forms from where you can import your items.

- If you have specific mentions you want to add in your Google forms and just want to inform the recipients and don't want to receive any response, you can do so using the **Tt** icon. Here, you can add title and description of your desired text.

- In case you want to add any image or video, you can do so using the 🖼 or ▶ icon. These can act as a supplement in your items. Sometimes, you might have noticed that people put the QR Code of their payment platform to receive payments for a specific seminar/ workshop.

- Sometimes, in conventional mode we see questions/ form with different sections, like Personal details, Educational Qualifications, Address etc. What if we want to make them in Google forms. We can do so using 🯰 icon. By clicking this we can separate sections and make the forms more user friendly.

- In online applications, some sections have * mark, which we can't skip and must fill it. Can we do this in Google Forms? Yes, we can. By just turning on the **Required** option.

- To delete an item, you can click on 🗑 icon of that specific item.

6.4. MANAGEMENT OF GOOGLE FORMS

SECTION-I: RESPONSES

1. Associating with Google Spreadsheet:

   As you collect responses from the participants, it becomes important to store them in a document form to analyse the data for remedial/ research purposes.

   This can be done using the 🔲 Link to Sheets option in the Responses section. Thereby, your forms and sheets will be synced with each other.

Along with this, you can also create new sheet at any time and sync the responses with the new one or you can select a specific folder in the Drive where you want to store the responses.

2. Accepting Responses:

Say you have scheduled a test using Google forms and it is of 10 minutes duration. In that case we can simply turn off the accepting responses option in the Responses section. Once you enable button respondents can again fill the form.

If there is any edit you want to do in the Forms, you can turn it off then as well.

SECTION-II: SETTINGS

1. Make this a Quiz

Once you enable this option, the forms can be evaluated (in case of selective type) automatically as well as after manual review of the responses (in case of subjective type). Thereafter, you can also enable on where the respondents were wrong and where the respondents performed well. Adding to this, you can also assign question wise marks in the form itself. Here, you can manually assign points to each item or make a specific point default in all the items in the form.

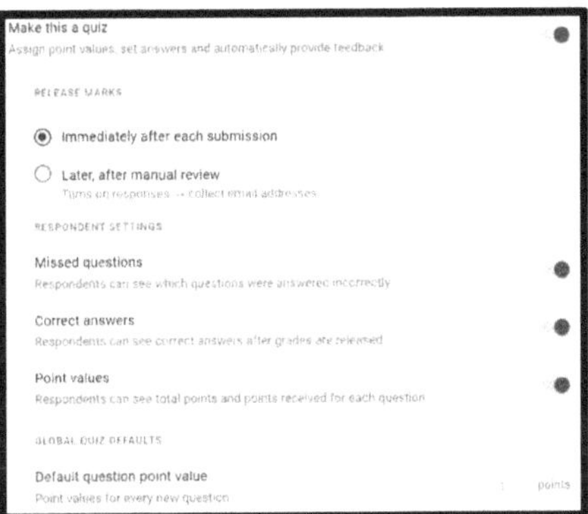

2. Responses

Here you can manage the responses you want to receive. You can also enable the form in such a manner that participants can attempt only once. The respondents can also edit their responses if the admin allows for it using the section below.

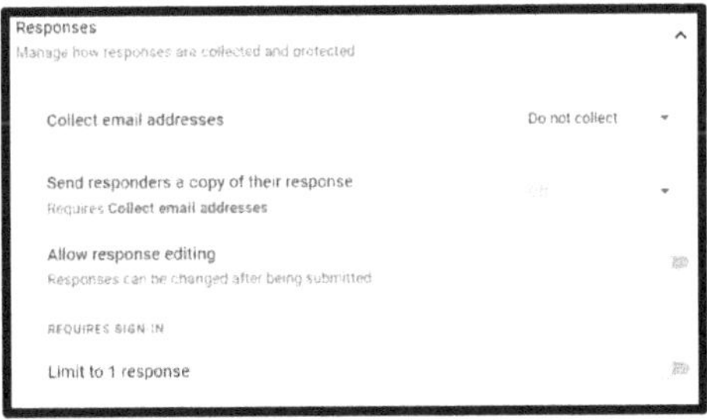

3. Presentation

Here, the administrator can edit on how the form will look to the respondents. In the **confirmation message option,** you can modify it with your own composed message. The other options are also useful in making the forms more creative.

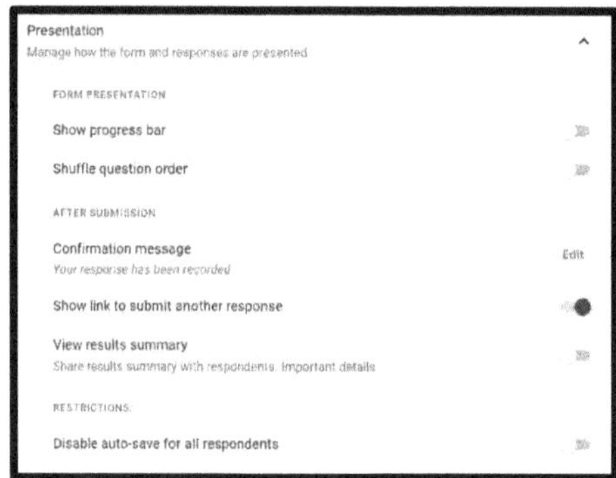

4. Form Defaults

The form default is the option where asking for e-mail addresses can be made default for all the respondents.

5. Question Defaults

Do you remember making the items required by clicking on the option. But all the options can be made as "required" by default using the option below.

6.5. SHARING GOOGLE FORMS

Google forms are to be sent for two distinct purposes. These include, sharing to get responses and sharing to become an editor.

1. **Sharing to get responses.**

As we have created the Google Forms, we are supposed to share to the recipients to get responses from them. The following options can be done to share the form with the recipients. The first step is to click on **Send** to send the form.

Option 1. Sharing As E-mail:

Click on the ✉ to send the form through e-mail. Enter the email address of the recipients and share the form with them directly.

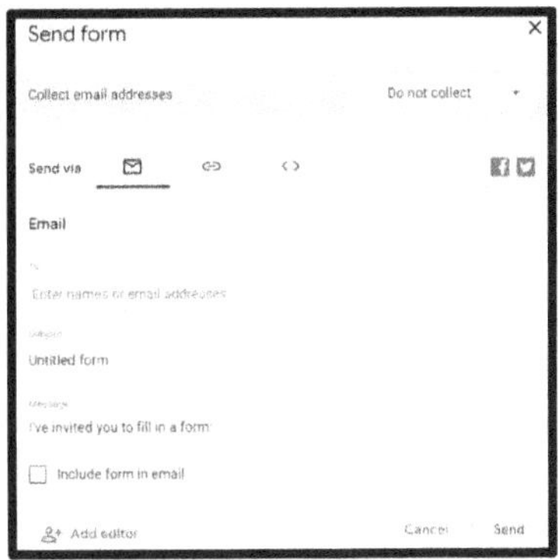

Option 2. Sharing As Link:

Click on 🔗 icon and you will see the detailed link of the form. You can simply copy the URL and paste it on any other messaging platform. However, you also have the option to make the URL of the form, you can also do so by using the checkbox below.

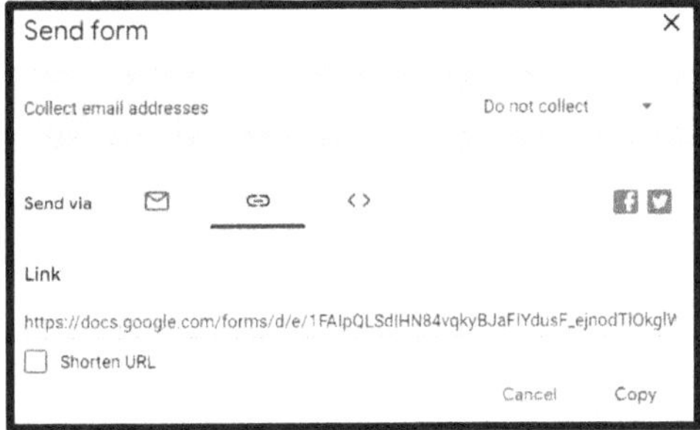

Option 3. Sharing As HTML:

Though it is not of much help, but you can also share the HTML with the recipients along with the option of sharing in your desired pixels. Then you can copy it and paste on your browser's desired location.

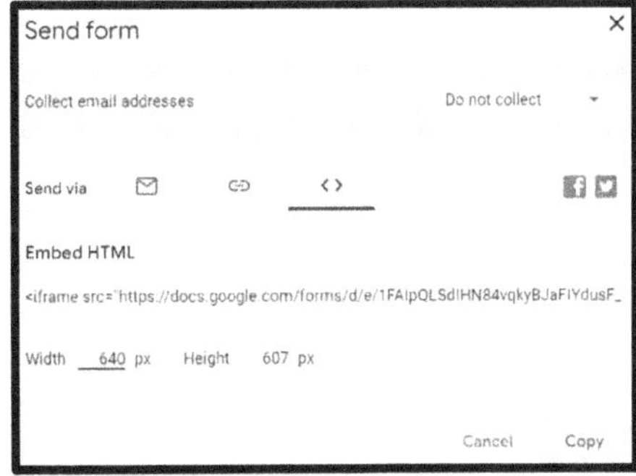

Option 4. Sharing Through Social Media Platforms:

The Google forms provides you with an in-built option of sharing it through Facebook or Twitter. You can directly share to those platforms if you have an active account there.

2. **Sharing to invite someone as editor.**

There are two options through which you can invite someone as editor.

Option 1. Through **Send** option

Click on ⵣ+**Add editor** and enter the required e-mail address and provide access to them as editor to the form.

Option 2. Through **Invite as a collaborator** option

Follow the same steps as above but from the option of **Invite as a collaborator** option available in the more options of the Google forms interface.

6.6. ADVANCED FEATURES OF GOOGLE FORMS

The advanced features of Google Forms simply mean adding the add-ons available on Google Forms through free or paid medium. Click on the following link to know more:

Adding Free Add-ons.

Besides, you can also follow the playlist below to know more about Google Forms.

1. Create a Google form to carry out a formative assessment of any of the subject you teach in the institute/ school in MCQ type with pre-defined scoring and share the Google form link along with its PDF in the following link.

   https://forms.gle/4kgEdygumtQLP63C6

2. Make the workshop coordinator as the collaborator and later proceed to make him/ her the admin of the forms and remove your participation from the form.

3. Collect data of 10 students on any test, export them to spreadsheet and sort them in alphabetical order in one sheet and in ascending order of their marks obtained in another sheet. Share the spreadsheet to the workshop coordinator using the inbuilt share option.

4. Make a Google form and send it to the workshop coordinator to fill. After that send them the automated certificate using the add-on provided in Google Forms.

5. Click on the following icon and check your understanding on Google Forms.

John R. Sowash. (2020, April 14). *Introduction to add-ons for Google Forms* [Video]. YouTube. https://www.youtube.com/watch?v=-jZPQpmOYws

The Tarrant Institute for Innovative Education. (2021, January 25). *How to Use Google Forms for assessment* [Video]. YouTube. https://www.youtube.com/watch?v=HPff8Zl-LTo

University of Wisconsin (2020, 16th June). *Google Forms: Creating, Editing, and Distributing*. https://www.uww.edu/documents/icit/documentation/google/icit-google%20forms.pdf

<u>ZOOM</u>

2.   MODULE CONTENTS:

2.1.   Module Objectives
2.2.   Introduction
2.3.   Creation of Zoom Account
2.4.   Introduction to Zoom Interface
2.5.   Hosting and Joining Zoom Meetings
2.6.   Advanced Features of Zoom

2.1.   MODULE OBJECTIVES

The teachers and teacher educators will be able to;

- Conceptualize the idea of Zoom.
- Create a Zoom account.
- Host or join a Zoom meeting.
- Use advanced features of Zoom.

2.2.   INTRODUCTION

During the COVID-19 pandemic the need for online learning, meetings, conferences have emerged in different sectors. In such a crisis, Zoom was the first company to have introduced the option of virtual meetings. It immediately became an application of worldwide concern where provision of online classes, meetings, conferences were being organized. Even at this date, Zoom is used widely in day-to-day lives to access from remote places.

Logo of Zoom

2.3.   CREATION OF ZOOM ACCOUNT

The first and foremost step is installing Zoom application in any electronic gadget you have. This will be followed by setting up the application on your gadget.

The next step is signing up in the Zoom. You can sign-in directly using available Apple/ Google/ Facebook account or manually enter your details.

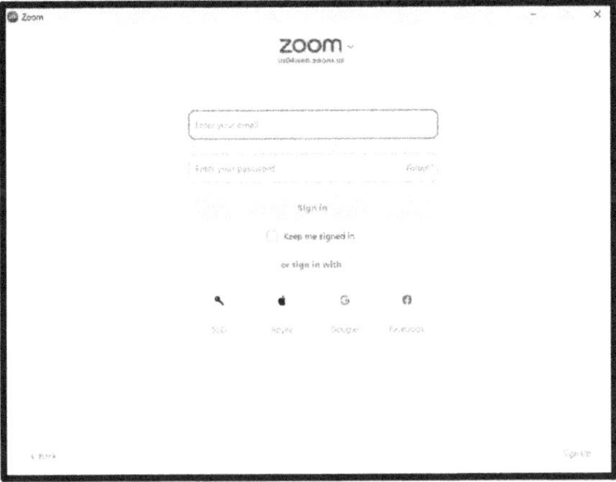

After this, you'll be required to enter further details.

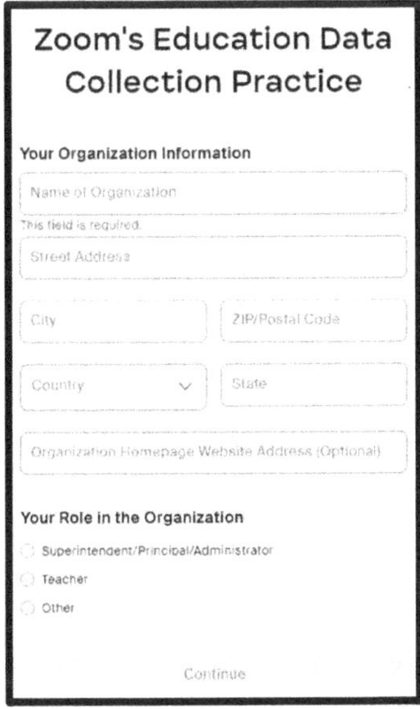

After you sign-in an interface like this will appear on your home page. Bravo, now you have successfully created your Zoom account.

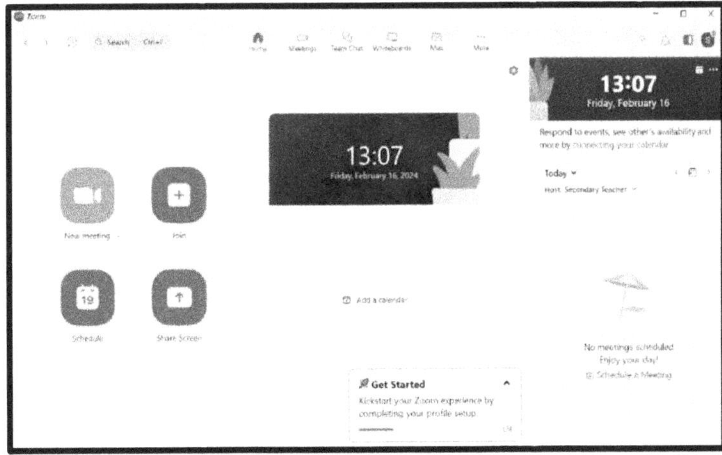

Here, you have different options available in the homepage of Zoom. These are,

⌂- Homepage of Zoom, under homepage you can see,

▭- To create new meeting (Either instant or by sending invitation for a later event).

⊞- To join a meeting using meeting ID.

▦- To schedule a meeting on a specific date using calendar.

⬆- To share screen directly by entering meeting ID.

▭- To view all the past and upcoming meetings.

💬- To start conversations/ chat with the members of the organization.

▭- To view all the whiteboards associated with your Zoom account.

✉- To e-mail using Zoom platform (Zoom account is available to premium users).

⚅- To add in-built apps like timer, group photo, virtual background, music etc. or additional apps.

⊟- To add/ create contact on Zoom.　　　　　　　▤- To sync calendar, like in Google.

⚙- To view/ edit the setting of Zoom.

2.4.　CREATION OF A ZOOM MEETING LINK

Creating a Zoom meeting link is similar to that of Google Meet. Click on the New Meeting icon on your Zoom application and you will directly enter into the video meeting.

New meeting ⌄

Other options in the drop-down menu of new meeting include,

- **Start with video.**
  This option enables you to start your video with the video mode on. However, you can later modify it inside the meeting as well.
- **Use my personal meeting ID.**
  This option lets you use your personal meeting ID to create meetings.
- **10- or 11-digit meeting ID**
  Under this option, you have 3 sub-options:
    - Copy ID- You can simply share the meeting ID through any e-mailing or messaging platform.
    - Copy invitation- Once you click it, you will have a proper paragraph on meeting invitation which can be shared using any e-mailing or messaging platform.
    - PMI Settings- To update personal meeting ID settings. These include video settings, audio settings, and some additional features.

2.5. ZOOM MEETING INTERFACE

This is what the Zoom interface looks like.

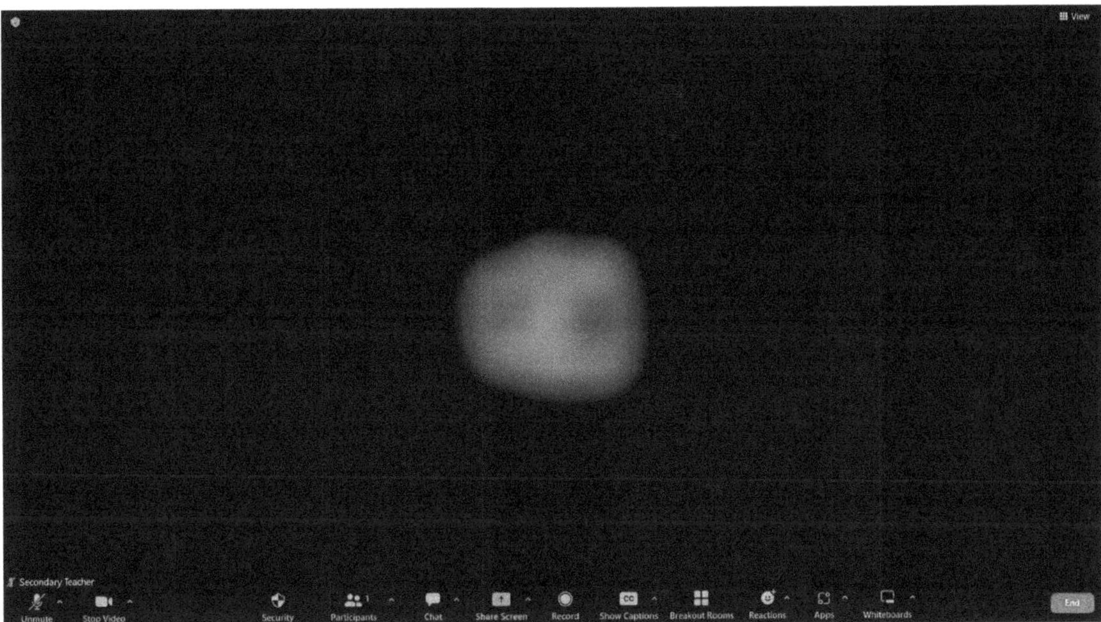

The common options between Google Meet and Zoom won't be discussed here. The options other than Meet include:

⦿- The record icon is unique to Zoom only. You can record the meeting up to 40 minutes in the basic plan i.e., the free version. The recording can be accessed from the meetings icon of the zoom, and it will also be saved on the host's device.

☺- The reactions icon is useful for participants to react to the event taking place in the meeting. Additionally, it allows participants to raise query by clicking on the option "Raise Hand".

⚇- This feature provides you option to use in-built and external apps. The in-built apps are available in my app section which include group photo, timer, virtual background, and music. The external apps are stored in "add apps" section. It includes AI based applications to enhance meeting experience, live streaming etc.

⬚ - This icon is to use white board during the meeting. Here you can opt to use new whiteboard or existing whiteboard to make the meeting more interactive and fruitful.

In case of smartphones, you will have additional option of Notes ▤. Here you can type your important points as note and it will be saved in the **More** option of the Zoom application installed on your smartphone.

Adding to this, every feature has a separate drop-down menu where you can manage the permissions and access in the meeting for the participants and the host.

1. Create a Zoom meeting link and share it as an invitation to the workshop co-ordinator through e-mail.
2. Take a note of the online workshop conducted using Zoom and share it with the workshop co-ordinator.
3. Attempt the questions provided by clicking on the link below.

https://forms.gle/Md5xHoDvXTtEAy1t8

Office of Information Technology (n.d.). *Zoom- Host a meeting and Invite Participants.* University of Colorado Boulder. https://oit.colorado.edu/tutorial/zoom-host-meeting-and-invite-participants

The University of North Carolina (n.d.). *How to Create a Zoom Account and Host a Meeting.* https://afirm.fpg.unc.edu/sites/afirm.fpg.unc.edu/files/covid-resources/How%20to%20Create%20a%20Zoom%20Account%20and%20Host%20a%20%20Meeting.pdf

------- (2022, 15 August). *Zoom: Advanced Features You Need to Know*. UC Today. https://www.uctoday.com/collaboration/zoom-advanced-features-you-need-to-know/

Division of Continuing Education (n.d.). *Zoom Training Advanced Tools and Features.* Harvard University.
https://projects.iq.harvard.edu/files/dcewebconf/files/zoomadvancedtrainingv2.4forsite.pdf